THE MUSEUMS OF PARIS

GREAT GALLERIES SERIES

THE MUSEUMS OF PARIS

Text by
RAYMOND CHARMET

MEREDITH PRESS · NEW YORK

First published in the United States in 1967
by Meredith Press
Des Moines and New York

Translated from the Italian
by
James Brockway

Printed in Italy for Meredith Press

In Paris, the visitor's attention is monopolized by the deserved fame of the Louvre, and accordingly many other remarkable museums, in which the capital is rich, are known to relatively few. Of the hundred odd of these which are open to the public there are at least thirty which are artistically of the first importance, as much for the magnificent architecture of the buildings which house them, as for the wealth of their collections.

Very varied in their history, purpose and contents, these museums can be classified into five categories.

The first category comprises those museums which act as a complement to the Louvre by putting on exhibition works of art from fields not represented at Paris largest museum. Thus the Musée du Jeu de Paume, which is actually attached to the Louvre, possesses masterpieces of impressionist painting, while painting and sculpture of a later period, of the 20th century, will be found at the National Museum of Modern Art (Musée National d'Art Moderne). Primitive art, of such great appeal today, ranging from that of Oceania in prehistoric times, to modern European folklore, will be found at the Museum of Man (Musée de l'Homme) and the popular arts of France at the Museum of Popular Arts and Traditions (Musée des Arts et Traditions Populaires). At the Guimet Museum, the visitor will encounter the various cultures of Central, Southern and Eastern Asia.

The museums belonging to the City of Paris itself should be included in this category, for in some respects their collections complete those of the national museums — the Petit Palais Museum, as regards the 19th century and the early years of the 20th, the Municipal Museum of Modern Art (Musée Municipal d'Art Moderne), as regards contemporary art, and the Cernuschi Museum, as regards the archæology of China.

In the second category we encounter certain aspects of art already represented at the Louvre, though not on such an extensive scale or so systematically arranged as here: medieval arts at the Cluny Museum, decorative arts at the Marsan Pavilion (Musée du Pavillon de Marsan), small exhibits in the Medals Room at the National Library (Cabinet des Médailles de la Bibliothèque Nationale), French sculpture at the French Monuments Museum (Musée des Monuments Français), where the collection naturally consists of casts and copies.

Some museums, falling into the third category, are devoted entirely to the artist whose name they bear and whose essential works are in their keeping. First among these are the great sculptors, Rodin and Bourdelle; then there are some painters, Delacroix, Gustave Moreau, Henner, and another name besides, too often forgotten in this field—that of Victor Hugo—all of whose drawings are collected in the Victor Hugo Museum in the Place des Vosges.

A fourth category is composed of collections belonging to rich connoisseurs, usually on display in their homes, which means that they have been preserved in the same atmosphere as that in which they were conceived. The most remarkable museum in this category—the Jacquemart-André Museum—contains masterpieces of Italian Renaissance art and 18th-century French works. Other museums in this category are the Cognacq-Jay, the Nissim de Camondo and the Marmottan Museums. A few other such collections have been brought under one roof in the Petit Palais.

Finally, a fifth series of Paris museums, including some highly important ones, is devoted to the story of certain of mankind's activities, such as the history of Paris (Carnavalet Museum), the Army (Les Invalides), the Navy, costumes, the tools and instruments of the arts and crafts, the opera, musical instruments, and the hospitals of Paris. Although the emphasis here is on the historical and social significance of the exhibits, these collections are not without aesthetic interest, thanks both to their possessing exhibits connected with great artists and to the quality of workmanship in earlier times.

Then there are the buildings in which all these museums are housed and which themselves constitute a most significant collection of examples of civil architecture, ranging from Roman times to the 20th Century. The Cluny Museum is partly housed in the sole surviving Roman building in the capital and partly in a most beautiful Gothic mansion. Part of the collections of the Museum of Arts and Crafts will be found in the church of Saint Martin-des-Champs, one of the purest examples of Romanesque ecclesiastical architecture. Important examples of 16th- and 17th-century architecture will be found in the Hôtel Carnavalet, the Victor Hugo Museum, the National Library and in the Hôtel des Miramiones, home of the Paris Hospitals Museum. The great masterpiece of late 17th-century architecture is, of course, the Hôtel des Invalides, a perfect setting for the War Museum. Among the elegant 18th-century town mansions (hôtels) now used as museum premises are: the Hôtel Soubise, home of the Museum of French History and the more discreet Hôtel Biron, in which the Rodin Museum is housed. These are two perfect examples of the classical style of French architecture.

The 19th-century is represented by the Jacquemart-André and the Gustave Moreau museums near the magnificent Paris Opera House, the interiors of which mansions afford the visitor an idea of the homes of the well-to-do of the time. As for the 20th-century, the Petit Palais is one of the most satisfying examples of turn of the century architecture, while the Palais de New York and the Palais de Chaillot, of 1937, show the evolution of modern architecture.

So it will be seen that a visit to the museums of Paris often allows access—otherwise difficult to obtain—to the most characteristic homes of the past, and this is not the least of their attractions.

THE MUSEUM OF IMPRESSIONISM (Musée de l'Impressionnisme), the only museum to bear the name of a school of painting, has been housed since 1947 in the Jeu de Paume pavilion, built in 1751 on the terrace of the Tuileries. During the inter-war period, this building, then known as the Musée du Jeu de Paume, housed works of contemporary artists of foreign nationality which are now on view at the National Museum of Modern Art. Extensive building operations between 1954 and 1958, carried out under the supervision of the keeper, Germain Bazin, have brought about a complete renovation of the premises, of the temperature control, air-conditioning, lighting and arrangement, in a manner whereby this building has become a wonderful example of modern museum technique.

Despite the museum's name, the painters represented there are not confined to the Impressionists proper, but also include their forerunners and the great late 19th-century innovators up to Van Gogh, Seurat and Henri Rousseau. Since the Impressionists were ostracized by the authorities of the day, the first of their masterpieces to go to the Luxembourg Museum, and later to the Louvre, were donations from important private collections; these works have been inherited by the present museum, itself a department of the Louvre. The famous collection assembled by the painter Caillebotte, bequeathed in 1883 and accepted, after the omission of 29 canvases, in 1886, comprised 67 works by the seven leading impressionist masters, including Manet's *The Balcony*, Renoir's *Le Moulin de la Galette* and *The Swing*, Monet's *La Gare Saint-Lazare* and Cézanne's *L'Estaque*. Bequeathed in 1908, the Isaac de Camondo donation, which was accepted particularly on account of the examples in 18th-century furniture it contained, added, together with numerous works by Degas, among them *Absinth* and *The Dancing Lesson*, works by Monet and Sisley and Cézanne's *Card Players*. In 1923 and 1927, Etienne Moreau-Nélaton offered the Louvre an important collection of modern paintings in which the Delacroix and Corots were sufficient to get some Monets accepted, some Pissarros and the celebrated *Déjeuner sur l'Herbe* by Manet, whose *Olympia* Clemenceau had persuaded the Louvre to accept in 1908, but only with difficulty.

Since the Second World War new donations have been added to the numerous acquisitions made by the authorities, who had in the meantime become more enlightened. Outstanding among these were the Paul Gachet donations of 1949, 1951 and 1954, whereby the museums acquired important Van Gogh canvases. In this way the museum has been enriched notably by paintings which Toulouse

The Cluny Museum (15th century).

Lautrec did for la Goulue's bar, by le Douanier Rousseau's *War*, numerous pieces of sculpture by Degas, including *The Little Dancing Girl,* and by fourteen of Gauguin's canvases, several of which came from the Matzukata Collection — reliefs in wood, with which the artist decorated his house in the South Pacific. Various panels giving information and documentary details have been erected in the centre of this museum, which has become a sanctuary of modern art.

THE NATIONAL MUSEUM OF MODERN ART (Musée National d'Art Moderne), which occupies three storeys of the right wing of the Palais de New York, built on the occasion of the International Exhibition of 1937, contains a large number of rooms, galleries and halls. Apart from important provisional exhibitions of contemporary French and foreign art, organized several times a year, this museum possesses large collections which, in 1964, comprised 4,281 paintings and 1,644 pieces of sculpture, a quarter of which are on exhibition, and also 3,309 aquarelles and drawings. The museum has a number of original features: its collection is constantly changing, since it relinquishes works after the hundredth anniversary of the artist's birth; the purchasing of its works by living artists is done by the Department of Arts and Literature, which hands on part of its purchases to the museum; and finally, it is one of the newest museums, having been inaugurated in 1947. It has taken the place of the Luxembourg Museum, which went back to 1818, and the former Jeu de Paume collection, which had been the home of works by foreign artists from 1920. Time, and more particularly the revolution in taste, has entirely transformed the nature of the collections, which were formerly based on a very outmoded tradition but now centre on the most advanced kinds of art, thanks to the initiative of the keepers, Jean Cassou, who left the museum in 1965, and Bernard Dorival, both of them renowned art historians.

Thus the Nabi Movement (Vuillard, Bonnard, Maurice Denis), the Fauves (Matisse, Derain, Marquet, Vlaminck) and the Cubists (Picasso, Braque, Juan Gris) are abundantly and felicitously

The Petit Palais Museum (1900).

represented, followed by the abstract movement (Kupka, Kandinsky, Bissière and Manessier — each of whom has a whole room to himself). Important posthumous donations have recently added to the museum's collections, notably those of Dufy and Delaunay in 1963. The painter, Dunoyer de Segonzac, has re-purchased his most significant canvases including *The Drinkers*, in order to offer them to the museum, which he did, also in 1963. The most recent bequest—that made by the Rouault heirs in 1964— comprises many hundreds of works left in the artist's studio on his death. The principal donations of works of sculpture were those of Despiau, of Brancusi, in 1961, whose entire studio has been reconstructed inside the museum, and of Pevsner, in 1964. It should be mentioned that a room reserved for the Naïfs bears the name of the critic, Wilhelm Uhde, who discovered and championed this group of painters.

Artists from abroad who have worked in Paris, from Vallotton and Van Dongen to Soutine, Picasso and Chagall, and the sculptor Zadkine too (he has an entire room to himself), are widely represented, so that the National Museum of Modern Art embraces, if not all 20th-century art, at least what is known as ' the Paris School.'

The municipal museums of the City of Paris possess important collections of modern art which happily complete the state's collections in some fields. The municipality's collections are arranged chronologically in two buildings. Painting and sculpture prior to 1914 are the subjects of the collections in the Petit Palais Museum, this building having been designed by Charles Girault for the 1900 Exhibition and decorated with ceilings by Albert Besnard and Maurice Denis. Numerous donators, ranging from Juliette Courbet, sister of the painter, to Théodore Duret, the critic, and

Ambroise Vollard, a merchant, have in turn enriched the museums collections, which are wholly unsystematized. Certain artists of the second half of the 19th century are represented in it by groups of works unrivalled by other museums, even the Louvre itself. One of these is Courbet, whose gallery is dominated by his celebrated painting, *Les Demoiselles de la Seine*. Another is Carpeaux, with an exceptionally rich series of works of sculpture and paintings. Still others include the sculptor, Dalou, the draughtsman, Constantin Guys, and a later artist, Odilon Redon, the symbolist painter. One room has been reserved for the official artists of the Third Republic, whose work is not to be seen elsewhere in Paris. Bonnard and Vuillard particularly are prominent among the remarkable series of paintings and decorations by 20th-century artists. This museum is under the direction of Mme S. Kahn, who succeeded André Chamson, the keeper who in the post-war years organized a series of exhibitions still talked about today. Exhibitions continue to be organized at the museum.

THE MUNICIPAL MUSEUM OF MODERN ART (Musée Municipal d'Art Moderne), which was opened in 1961 in the left wing of the Palais de Tokyo and is the newest of the Paris museums, contains painting and sculpture since 1914. Its pride is the collection bequeathed by a Dr Girardin, who died in 1951, and which comprises 80 Rouaults, 110 Gromaires, 23 Maria Blanchards, 18 Dufys and 13 canvases by Buffet, the painter he discovered and launched. With its fifteen rooms, and containing also, in a special rotunda, Raoul Dufy's *Electricity*—the largest of contemporary paintings, executed in 1937—this museum offers the visitors a judicious selection of the works of contemporary artists, less concentrated on the avant-garde than is the National Museum of Modern Art, to which it acts as a useful counterweight.

THE MUSEUM OF MAN (Musée de l'Homme) occupies the major part of the Passy wing of the Palais de Chaillot, which was designed for the International Exhibition of 1937 by the architects, Carlu, Boileau and Azéma. Heir of the Ethnographical Museum in the former Trocadéro and of the museum's Anthropological Gallery, this vast museum, unique in France, demonstrated the activities and creative achievements of the primitive civilization in all ages and all regions of the world.

The museum is therefore mainly educative and scientific in character, the exhibits being arranged according to region, subject and techniques. But in view of the great interest the primitive arts arouse today, the most has also been made of the works of sculpture in the museum's keeping, which are often quite remarkable and constitute its chief riches. Thus, side by side with exhibits illustrating the evolution of the human species, the prehistoric section has on display the celebrated ivory Venus of Lespugue and that of Laugerie-Basse. There are a large number of pieces which come from America in the pre-Spanish era and represent one of the world's leading collections, its rarest jewel being the Aztec skull in rock crystal. The sections devoted to the art of Negro Africa and Oceania likewise contain some remarkable items, including bronzes, wooden masks, basketwork and two very large and impressive stone statues from Easter Island. The accent in other sections, devoted to the primitive arts of white Africa, Asia, Europe, the USSR and the Arctic regions, is laid to a greater extent on folklore. The latest room to be added to the museum, devoted to arts and techniques, takes one up to 1960.

With M. Millet, who teaches anthropology at the museum, at its head, the Musée de l'Homme is a busy centre of research, possessing a dozen departments of science equipped with their own laboratories, and also a vast library of photographs, a department devoted to the ethnology of music, an ethnographical film committee and several learned societies.

THE MUSEUM OF POPULAR ARTS AND TRADITIONS (Musée des Arts et Traditions Populaires), which is likewise accommodated in the Palais de Chaillot, completes the collections of the Museum of Man as regards the ethnography of France. Its considerable collections are not on permanent exhibition but are put on display in the form of temporary exhibitions. They embrace all modes of the nation's traditions, including homes, costumes, tools, trades, pastimes, beliefs. The museum works highly systematically to put on exhibition the results of research done in the laboratory of French Ethnography, under the direction of the keeper, G. H. Rivière. The various aspects and the creative achievements—works often of an extraordinary beauty—of modes of life now rapidly disappearing in France have been exhibited in this way. At the moment, a huge modern build-

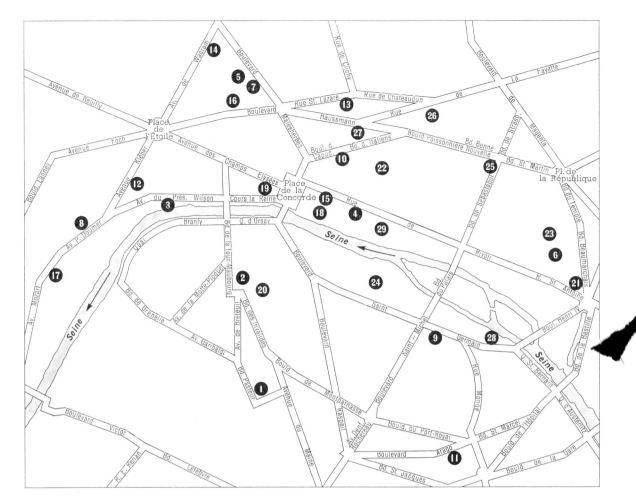

Map of Paris, showing the location of the museums described in this volume.

1. Bourdelle Museum, 16, Rue Antoine-Bourdelle
2. War Museum, Hôtel des Invalides, Esplanade des Invalides
3. Palais de New York (National Museum of Modern Art, Municipal Museum of Modern Art, Costumes Museum), 14, Avenue du Président Wilson
4. Museum of Decorative Arts, 107, Rue de Rivoli (1 pm to 7 pm, except Tuesdays; 11 am to 6 pm on Sundays)
5. Nissim de Camondo Museum, 63, Rue de Monceau (2 pm to 5 pm, except Tuesday; closed during July)
6. Carnavalet Museum, 23, Rue de Sévigné.
7. Cernuschi Museum, 7, Avenue Vélasquez
8. Palais de Chaillot (Museum of Man, Maritime Museum, French Monuments Museum, Museum of Popular Arts and Traditions), Place du Trocadéro
9. Cluny Museum, 6, Place Paul Painlevé

10. Cognacq-Jay Museum, 25, Boulevard des Capucines
11. Gobelins Museum, 42, Avenue des Gobelins
12. Guimet Museum, 6, Place d'Iéna
13. Gustave Moreau Museum, 14, Rue La Rochefoucauld
14. Jean-Jacques Henner Museum, 43, Avenue de Villiers (2 pm to 5 pm, except Mondays)
15. Museum of Impressionism, Place de la Concorde
16. Jacquemart-André Museum, 158, Boulevard Haussmann
17. Marmottan Museum, 2, Rue Louis Boilly (Sundays and Saturdays, 2 pm to 5 pm; closed in July and August)
18. Orangery Museum, 9, Place de la Concorde
19. Petit Palais, Avenue Dutuit
20. Rodin Museum, 77, Rue de Varenne (1 pm to 5 pm, except Tuesdays)

21. Victor Hugo Museum, 6, Place des Vosges (10 am to 12 noon and 2 pm to 6 pm, except Tuesdays)
22. Medals Room, National Library, 58, Rue de Richelieu (9.30 am to 12 noon and 1.30 pm to 4.45 pm, except Sundays)
23. French History Museum, 60, Rue des Francs-Bourgeois (2 pm to 5 pm, except Tuesdays)
24. Delacroix Museum, 6, Place Furstenberg
25. National Conservatory of Arts and Crafts, 292, Rue Saint-Martin (1.30 pm to 5.30 pm, except Mondays)
26. Musical Instruments Museum, 14, Rue de Madrid (Thursday and Saturday, 2 pm to 4.30 pm; closed from 15 July to 10 October)
27. Opera Museum, Théâtre de l'Opéra, Rue Auber
28. Paris Hospitals Museum, 47, Quai de la Tournelle

Unless otherwise stated, these museums are open every day, except Tuesdays, from 10 am to 12 noon and from 2 pm to 5 pm.

ing, destined to be the museum's new home, is in the course of construction on the site of the former Palm Garden, at the Zoo in the Bois de Boulogne.

THE GUIMET MUSEUM (Musée Guimet) has, since 1945, performed the official function of the National Museum's Department of Asiatic Art. As such, it has inherited works from the former museum at Lyons, which was founded by Emile Guimet in 1879 and transferred to Paris in 1885, only works of lesser importance remaining in Lyons. It also contains further Asiatic collections from the Louvre and some original pieces from the former Indo-Chinese Museum in the Trocadéro, which had been founded in 1878 by Louis Delaporte.

Its collections have also been considerably enriched with the fruits of searches performed by French schools in Asia. Its character has been entirely transformed, the merely picturesque and exotic having been abandoned for archeology and the great art of the civilizations of East, Central and Southern Asia. The most remarkable section of the museum, that of Khmer art, which is the finest collection of its kind outside Cambodia, owes its development mainly to the work carried out by the French Far East School. It was reorganized by Philippe Stern, an eminent expert on this art, who has since been succeeded as keeper of the museum by Mlle Jeannine Auboyer.

The principal sources of supply as regards the Greco-Buddhist art of Afghanistan have been the Foucher and Hackin expeditions, and as regards Tibet, the Jacques Bacot collection, which was put on exhibition once again in 1964. The arts of China and Japan, the great periods of which are well represented here, have benefited, as far as ceramic ware is concerned, from the Grandidier and Koechlin collections, and, as regards prints, from the Camondo Fund. Endowed with a vast library of books, a photographic and a record library, the Guimet Museum is the seat of many learned societies and has an annexe in the Avenue d'Iéna (no. 19), which houses a department of religious studies at which temporary exhibitions are held.

THE CERNUSCHI MUSEUM (Musée Cernuschi), situatedn ear the parc Monceau and bequeathed to the City of Paris by the collector whose name it bears in 1895, also contains works which illustrate the archeology of China. Relatively few in number, these items are of very high quality indeed. At

The National Museum of Modern Art (1937).

this same museum one can see—thanks to the Kou-Yushou donation—the only collection of contemporary Chinese painting on show in Paris.

THE CLUNY MUSEUM (Musée de Cluny) is housed in the Des Thermes building (the old Roman Baths) and the former mansion of the Abbés de Cluny. The first edifice, which goes as far back as the second century A. D., or the beginning of the third century A. D., contains the only ancient Roman vaulted hall to have survived in France. It is 45 ft. high. The second building, constructed between 1485 and 1498, with its sculpted windows and its chapel, is one of the most beautiful examples of the flamboyant style of architecture in the country. In 1833, a curious personage, one Alexandre Du Sommerard, a kind of Cousin Pons, accumulated whimsical collections of his own in the mansion and these, together with the house, he bequeathed to the state in 1843. A small room in the museum still preserves his memory. The Museum of National Antiquities, conceived by Alexandre Lenoir in 1833, was opened there in 1844. It was in 1920 that the museum, whose collections had in the meantime expanded on an enormous scale, exceeding 20,000 items, was attached to the Objets d'Art department of the Louvre. It was entirely reorganized by its keepers, Pierre Verlet and Francis Salet, thirteen rooms being re-opened in 1949 and ten more in 1956, devoted, apart from some Gallo-Roman exhibits, to the arts and crafts of the Middle Ages.

Sculpture, gold and silverware, enamelling and joinery are amply represented. But the museum's chief treasure is its collection of tapestries, especially the 'La Vie Seigneuriale' series, purchased in Normandy in 1852, and the famous 'La Dame à la Licorne' (The Lady with the Unicorn) series, purchased at Bussac in 1882.

Courtyard of the Carnavalet Museum.

THE MUSEUM OF DECORATIVE ARTS (Musée des Arts Décoratifs), founded by the Central Society of the Decorative Arts, a private body, was housed in the Palace of Industry in 1882, before being transferred to the Marsan Pavilion (a wing of the Louvre) in 1905, where its collections, comprising some 45,000 items, all state property, fill four immense floors. Exceedingly rich in composition, the collections embrace almost all the arts of all countries since Gothic times, finding room for complete reconstructions of ancient interiors, arranged, where possible, chronologically. There have been a very large number of bequests, of which one may mention those by Emile Peyre (the Middle Ages and the Renaissance), by Doisteau (porcelain), by the Comte de Rambuteau (books), by H. E. Perrin (18th century works) and by J. Maciet (Mussulman art), the last-mentioned being lavishly represented, especially as regards carpets. The museum also has something to offer which will not be found elsewhere—rooms devoted to the art of 1900. On the ground floor, important exhibitions—especially of contemporary art—are organized from time to time and assure the Society—and thus the museum as well—of adequate sources of income.

THE MEDALS ROOM (Cabinet des Médailles) at the National Library is a discreet collection of rarely visited treasures. Reaching far into the past, in fact, to the 16th century, and enriched by donations made during the course of four hundred years, this collection contains 400,000 coins and medals, the richest known collection of cameos and intaglios, the famous Throne of Dagobert, collections of antique silver-plate, the Egyptian items in the Caylus collection, very rare Sassanid wine cups, without rival in the Louvre. The museum contains, in fact, costly small objets d'art of all periods.

THE FRENCH MONUMENTS MUSEUM (Musée des Monuments Français), on the other hand, has the larger manifestations of art on display—but in the form of reproductions, of course. An inspiration of Viollet-de-Duc, who broached the idea of such a museum in 1879, and opened to the public in 1882 as the Museum of Comparative Sculpture at the Trocadéro, it was transferred, in 1937, after the Trocadéro's demolition, to the Palais de Chaillot and completely remodelled. Today one can see in it monumental sculpture from the 12th to the 19th century and also, since 1945, reproductions of Roman and Gothic frescoes, which have been added step by step.

THE FRENCH HISTORY MUSEUM (Musée de l'Histoire de France) is of minor significance only as regards works of art, having on display only items of historical interest, parchments, seals—though these include some very beautiful specimens. The building in which it is housed, however, l'Hôtel Soubise, constructed between 1705 and 1719 by the architect Delamair and comprising the Hôtel Clisson, dating from the 14th century, is one of the finest edifices in the whole of Paris, the interior decoration—especially that designed by Boucher, Natoire and Van Loo—being of great refinement.

THE RODIN MUSEUM (Musée Rodin), in which the works of this genius are preserved, is housed in the quietest and most harmonious of 18th century Paris mansions. Built between 1727 and 1729 by the architects Jacques Gabriel and Jean Aubert, for Peyrenc de Moras, a rich wig-maker, it acquired the name of Hôtel de Biron in 1753 from its third owner, an army marshall, who had succeeded the Duchess of Maine. In 1904, after housing for seventy-five years a school for young ladies, the building became the property of the state, which put it at the disposal of artists and poets: Matisse, Isadora Duncan, Jean Cocteau and Rainer Maria Rilke. In 1910 the last of these invited Rodin there and after submitting a petition Rodin eventually obtained an agreement (in 1916) whereby he was allowed to occupy the entire house on condition that he bequeathed his works and collections to the state. After Rodin's death in 1917, Léonce Bénédite was put in charge of the renovation of the building and the museum's organization. It contains the sculptor's complete works, bronzes, marbles and drawings, installed in the mansion and the adjacent chapel. There are a number of celebrated pieces in the garden too, including *The Thinker*, returned, in 1922, from the Panthéon, where it had been placed in 1906. During the tourist season, Mme Goldscheider, the museum's active curator, organizes exhibitions of contemporary sculpture there. The artist's private collection contains works from ancient Egypt, Greece and Rome, and also some unexpected canvases by Van Gogh *(Le Père Tanguy)*, Renoir, Monet and Carrière.

The Palais de Chaillot, home of several museums, seen from the Eiffel Tower.

THE BOURDELLE MUSEUM (Musée Bourdelle) is housed in a 19th century artist's home consisting of studios and small pavilions situated in the nowadays out-of-the-way quarter of Maine. The illustrious sculptor settled there on his arrival in Paris in 1884, living there till his death in 1929. His wife offered the house to the state, which declined the offer, and then to the municipality of Paris, which, being better advised, accepted, acquiring the site, the studios, and 876 original sculptures, 1,500 drawings and aquarelles, 100 paintings, pastels and frescoes and the master's manuscripts. After a series of re-organizations in keeping with the character of these rooms, so redolent of the artist's life there, it was possible to open a well-arranged museum in 1949. Some enlargements followed, the principal one being the construction, in 1961, of a gallery, 130 ft. long and 35 ft. high, to contain the master's more monumental statuary. Periodic exhibitions of Bourdelle's work, based on various themes, and of the work of other modern sculptors are regularly organized at the museum.

THE DELACROIX MUSEUM (Musée Delacroix) is a small, rather modest museum, the entrance of which gives on to the charming square, Place Furstenberg. Its premises are the house in which the artist lived during the last years of his life, from 1857 to August 13, 1863. His apartments and studio, acquired in 1952 by the Friends of Delacroix Society, which gave them to the National Museums, have been arranged as a museum, containing personal and iconographical reminders of the artist and his family, and some canvases of his own, and his contemporaries' work. A fair number of works by Delacroix entrusted to the museum by the Louvre give it indisputable interest. During the spring and summer months exhibitions are organized at the museum based on themes relevant to Delacroix and his circle.

THE GUSTAVE MOREAU MUSEUM (Musée Gustave Moreau) had become almost forgotten, until a large exhibition was held at the Louvre in 1961. A sudden vogue among followers of the avant-garde re-focussed interest upon this academic and symbolist painter. He had lived in this town-house, until he died there in 1896, leaving it to the state together with his collections, which comprised a thousand paintings, including the majority of his own most famous works and over 7,000 drawings and sketches. The luxurious appointment of these rooms, which Georges Rouault, Moreau's faithful disciple, was careful to preserve as the museum's keeper, gives a good idea of the interior of an 'artist painter's' home in the 19th century style.

THE JEAN-JACQUES HENNER MUSEUM (Musée Jean-Jacques Henner), today quite deserted, is housed in the home where this painter died in 1905 and which his heirs bequeathed to the state in 1925. Here, in these sombre rooms, will be found works from every phase of the artist's career, originating from his studio and his house at Bernwiller in Alsace. *Sic transit...*

THE VICTOR HUGO MUSEUM (Musée Victor Hugo), in a corner of the splendid Place des Vosges, formerly the Place Royale, occupies a two-storey apartment where the poet lived between 1832 and 1848. The interior has been changed considerably since then by the schools which used the building after 1862. However, on the occasion of the centenary of Hugo's birth in 1902, the Paris municipality, which owned the premises, decided to set up this museum there. Paul Maurice, a great friend of the author and his executor, offered an exceptionally fine collection of his drawings, furniture, books and souvenirs. The museum was opened to the public on June 30, 1903. As time passed the collection was enlarged and so too was the accommodation, the museum now occupying the neighbouring premises as well. Raymond Escholier, the keeper between 1913 and 1933, had the collection arranged in a perfect manner, with an historical department on the first floor and a more personal collection on the second, where, for example, one can see the furniture Hugo designed together with 339 washes and drawings which reveal his great artistic gifts.

THE JACQUEMART-ANDRÉ MUSEUM (Musée Jacquemart-André), the property of the Institut de France, represents Paris's finest example of a collection of masterpieces assembled at the end of the 19th century, by an extremely wealthy connoisseur who installed them in his own luxurious Paris home. The building itself was erected between 1869 and 1875, according to designs submitted by the architect, Henri Parent, to the collector, Edouard André, a banker's son and former army officer. In 1881 he married Nélie Jacquemart, a fashionable painter. They built up their collections, travelling in Italy and purchasing among other works three Tiepolo frescoes, the only ones to be seen in Paris. After Edouard André's death in 1894, his wife continued to add to the collections and organized her 'Italian museum' on the first floor. On her death, in 1912, she bequeathed her fortune, her home and its art treasures to the Institut de France. The living apartment and reception rooms, splendidly decorated with tapestries, furniture and ancient objets d'art, have been preserved in their original state. As for the collections, these are concentrated in the main on the Italian Renaissance and the 18th century in France, but also include masterpieces which have come down to us from other centuries, notably some Rembrandts and the celebrated *Heures de Boucicaut*. In recent years, prior to his death, J. G. Domergue organized some brilliant exhibitions devoted to Van Gogh, Toulouse-Lautrec and Goya in the museum—exhibitions which attracted all Paris.

THE COGNACQ-JAY MUSEUM (Musée Cognacq-Jay), bequeathed to the City of Paris, commemorates the names of Ernest Cognacq and his wife, Marie-Louise Jay. This museum was installed in the luxury store of La Samaritaine, in order to comply with the wishes of the founder, and donator Ernest Cognacq who died in 1928. Cognacq wished to see assembled in one place the works he had collected with so much love during his last years. A number of fairly small rooms, spread over three floors, bring together furniture, porcelain, figurines, jewels and, above all, 18th century paintings and drawings in an atmosphere of quiet intimacy, constituting a homogeneous collection of great taste. The twelve drawings by Watteau and the eight gouaches by Millet, among other items, make a most valuable addition to the other museums.

THE NISSIM DE CAMONDO MUSEUM (Musée Nissim de Camondo) is housed in a mansion in the parc Monceau, built between 1911 and 1914 by Sergent, in the 18th century style which was then so popular. The name the museum bears is that of the son of the donator, the Comte Moïse de Camondo, a cousin of Isaac de Camondo, who left some impressionist canvases to the Louvre. Inaugurated on December 21, 1936 and bequeathed to the Central Society of Decorative Arts, this museum is of interest to students of the applied arts of the 18th century by virtue of the extreme richness of its furniture, including items which bear the signatures of some of the great cabinet-makers, 23 Aubusson and Savonnerie tapestries and a rich collection of Chinese porcelain.

THE MARMOTTAN MUSEUM (Musée Marmottan) was entrusted in 1932 to the Institut de France by Paul Marmottan, the author and art historian, son of Jules Marmottan, the Director of Mines at Bruay, for the purpose of preserving intact the collections built up by his father and himself. These collections are partly concerned with the German and Spanish primitives and for another and more important part with the First Empire, a period most collectors tend to overlook but which is represented here in the form of some very choice items of furniture, objets d'art and paintings. Besides these, there is a room one would hardly expect to find, containing recent bequests by Donop de Monchy, where some excellent impressionist paintings are to be seen, including Claude Monet's famous *Impression: soleil levant*, which title caused a spiteful critic to give this school of painting the name which all the world has since come to know and respect.

THE DUTUIT AND THE EDWARD TUCK COLLECTIONS. Mention should be made of these two private collections which, placed in the keeping of museums, have so far been preserved intact. Both are to be found at the Petit Palais. The first is the Dutuit Collection, formed by the brothers Eugène and Auguste Dutuit and bequeathed in 1902, the catalogue of which contains 1593 items, as wide in range as they are rich. They range from antiques to Dutch painting, including a splendid Rembrandt, the *Self-Portrait with a Dog*, and from Limoges enamels to medals by Pisanello. The other, the Edward Tuck Collection, donated in 1930, contains primitive works, Beauvais tapestries, and Chinese black porcelain.

THE CARNAVALET MUSEUM (Musée Historique de la Ville de Paris) takes pride of place among the historical museums, as much by virtue of its collections—for which twenty-four rooms are nowadays insufficient—as by virtue of the wealth of memories which they evoke.

Begun in 1544 by Pierre Lescot and Jean Goujon, the building still preserves statuary by the latter in its courtyard. It was in 1572 that it acquired its name, from the second occupier, the widow of a Monsieur de Kernevenoy, from which the French made 'Carnavalet.' But its most illustrious owner was Mme. de Sévigné, who lived there from 1676 to her death in 1696. A room in the mansion still preserves her memory and some of her furniture. There is a bronze (1689) of Louis XIV, Coysevox's masterpiece, which formerly stood in the courtyard of the Paris Hôtel de Ville.

The city acquired the mansion in 1866 and set up the museum in the premises in 1880, considerably enlarging it in 1914. Two annexes were added, one between 1905 and 1914 along the rue de

Les Invalides — Home of the War Museum.

Sévigné, the other between 1910 and 1915 along the rue Payenne. The addition of the Hôtel Lepeletier de Saint-Fargeau, at present housing the Historical Library of the City of Paris, is under consideration.

The collections on exhibition illustrate the history of Paris, from the 16th century to this day, life at all levels of society and public events. Some very fine old collections have been transferred to the museum and re-assembled there, among the items being the Great Chamber of the Hôtel de La Rivière from the place Royale, with a ceiling by Le Brun, Louis XV wainscoting from the Premonstrant convent in the rue Hautefeuille and the Louis XVI circular drawing-room from the Hôtel Fersen.

THE COSTUMES MUSEUM (Musée du Costume) is an important department of the City of Paris Historical Museum, which was transferred to an annexe at the Palais de New York some time ago. Here historical costumes are put on display by means of a series of exhibitions showing various items from the collection.

THE WAR MUSEUM (Musée de l'Armée). This museum is housed in the long galleries of the Hôtel des Invalides, the most majestic of the edifices Louis XIV had raised in Paris. It was built by Libéral Bruant between 1671 and 1676, but Hardouin-Mansart was the designer of the domed chapel (Chapelle du Dôme), which was consecrated in 1706. The present museum was formed in 1905 by amalgamating the Artillery Museum (Musée de l'Artillerie), inaugurated in 1794, with the Historical Museum (Musée Historique), founded in 1896. It comes under the jurisdiction of the Ministry of War. The arms and armour, first kept in the Bastille by order of Louis XIV, contain 15th- and 16th-century items of exceptional value. Outstanding items in the museum's collection of paintings are Van der Meulen's canvases of towns conquered in 1677 and a large portrait of Napoleon I on his throne, painted by Ingres in 1806 by order of the Legislative Council.

THE MARITIME MUSEUM (Musée de la Marine) acquired galleries worthy of its collection in the Palais de Chaillot, after having had to be content with small, dimly-lit rooms at the Louvre until 1938. It has immense reserves of exhibits, 28,000 photos of objects and documents in its collections, illustrating all sections of shipping, models, often of large dimensions, and former royal vessels, which are true works of art.

Among the numerous paintings in the museum's possession are the French ports series, large canvases done by Joseph Vernet from 1752 onwards at the official request of the Marquis de Marigny.

THE NATIONAL CONSERVATORY OF ARTS AND CRAFTS (Conservatoire National des Arts et Métiers) is housed in what was formerly the priory of Saint-Martin-des-Champs. Here one will find a very beautiful 12th century church, a 13th century refectory, and 18th century buildings, enlarged between 1845 and 1891. The Conservatory owes its foundation, in 1795, to the Directoire (the Supreme Executive Council), acting upon a proposal made by the Abbé Grégoire. It traces the entire history of mechanics and machines. The main artistic interest of the museum lies in its collection of glassware, a highly remarkable collection of clocks and watches occupying two rooms, and its automata.

THE MUSICAL INSTRUMENTS MUSEUM (Musée Instrumental) has a collection of instruments of a different kind, housed in the Conservatory of Music. The latter possesses about 2,000 items built up from the collection of Clapisson, the composer (1808-1866), who was the museum's founder. The majority of these antique instruments are of great historical interest. Artistically, they are of the highest order.

THE OPERA MUSEUM (Musée de l'Opéra) is a small museum, though an exceedingly interesting one, attached to the 'grand théâtre lyrique' in Paris. It contains documentary material on all the theatrical productions since its foundation in 1669; also a fine series of portraits of musicians and instrumentalists, including Renoir's portrait of Wagner, presented to the museum by Alfred Cortot. The museum is to be enlarged to include a ballet museum.

THE PARIS HOSPITALS MUSEUM (Musée des Hôpitaux de Paris) is an original and highly engaging museum housed, since 1934, in the quai de la Tournelle, in the Hôtel des Miramiones, a 17th century edifice which after 1810 became the 'Hôtel de la Pharmacie centrale des Hôpitaux.' Its collections are devoted to medicine, surgery, pharmacy and hospitalization, illustrated by means of documents and curiosities, including a collection of 647 pharmacists' bowls, as used through the ages.

Thus all the arts in their most diverse aspects, from the noblest to the humblest, are there to be studied and admired in the museums of the City of Paris.

Easter Island Head. Volcanic tufa. Height: 1.85 m. Museum of Man.

This statue was brought to France by the expeditionary vessel, *Flore*, in 1872. Pierre Loti, then a midshipman, supervised the work of sawing and transporting it. First kept in the National History Museum and transferred in 1930 to the Ethnographical Museum, it is now in the Musée de l'Homme. Easter Island has a large number of these gigantic heads, whose origin in such isolated and denuded parts remains obscure. The effect they make, perched on high, their backs turned to the sea, is exceedingly strange and fantastic.

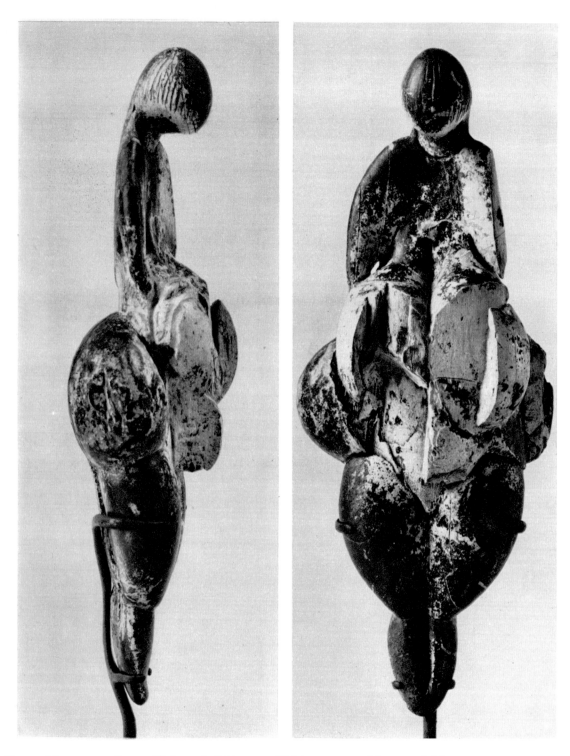

Venus of Lespugue. Bone. Higher paleolithic age. Height: 15 cm. Museum of Man.

Discovered in a cave in Haute-Garonne, this statuette is regarded as the masterpiece of paleolithic sculpture, going back to between forty and twenty thousand years before Christ. Like several analogous pieces, it is steatopygic, that is to say, broad-buttocked. But it is distinguished from all other examples by virtue of the delicate neck, slender arms, a net garment covering the legs at the back, and, above all, by the genuine artistic style with which the volumes have been harmonized — the sign of a conscious artist.

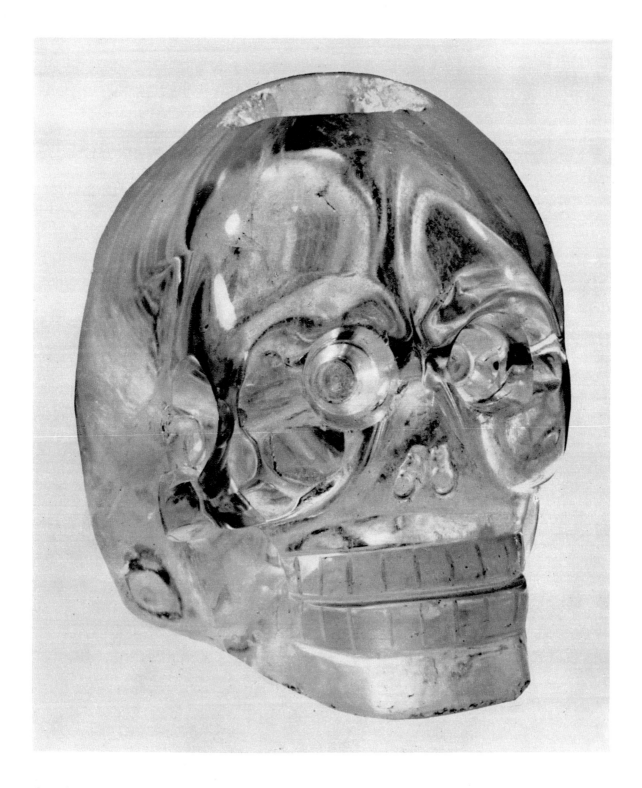

Skull in rock crystal. Mexico. 14th-15th century. Height: 11 cm. Museum of Man.

A work of Aztec or Mixtec culture, this piece bears witness to the death cult which obsessed the early Mexicans. Coatlicue, their Earth Goddess, venerated as being the source from which all things emanated, shows by her fleshless head that the Earth is at one and the same time a nourisher and a devourer of life. The realistic style, making bold use of smooth surfaces, confers on the head a hallucinatory character.

On right: *Tiki. Black lava. Marquesas Islands. Height: 15 cm. Museum of Man.*
On left: *Double Tiki. Of similar provenance. On loan to the Museum of Man.*

In Oceania, Tiki is a god of virility and fertility shown in human form, sometimes of large dimension but more often small. The head is massive and without a neck, the mouth is slightly open and shows the tongue, the body is thick-set. It will be found (in wood) in all objects of common use, to render them effective. In statuette form, whether in the single or double version, these Tikis are of great plastic and expressive power, putting them in the very first rank of Oceanic sculpture.

Head of Idol. Basket-work. Hawaii Islands. Height: 1 m. Museum of Man.

Decorated with feathers, with real teeth in its mouth and mother of pearl eyes, this figure displays those elements of caricature, violent expressiveness, terror and sarcasm in Oceanic art which have proved so attractive to avant-garde artists, particularly to the surrealists. Previously regarded simply as items of ethnographical interest, these statues have since been promoted to the rank of high art.

Male Statuette. Dark wood. New Guinea. Height: 30 cm. (Front and profile). Museum of Man.

This curious figurine, sculpted from wood, painted, adorned with fibre and a *tapa*, represents Ramu, one of the New Guinean ancestors. The stylization, with the elongated, bent nose is characteristic of New Guinea.

Pendant Mask. Bronze. Southern Nigeria. Height: 20 cm. Museum of Man. ▶

The art of the Benin region, which goes back as far as the 15th century, has produced the finest bronzes of Negro Africa. It is distinguished from the other Negro arts by its striving towards, a classical realism.

Statue of the God Gou. Iron. Dahomey.
Height: 1.65 m. Museum of Man.

Gou is the God of Arms and War.
Of unusual size and constructed entirely of iron, this statue strikes one
with the strange fascination of some
figure in a ballet and with the air of
magic conferred upon it by its separ-
ate elements.

Nimba, Goddess of Maternity. Wood and fibre. Guinea. Height: 2 m. Museum of Man.

It is the Baga tribe which has created this type of mask, of huge dimensions, which is worn at rituals and designed to protect pregnant women. Its ornamentation in the form of lines of nails, the marked but highly eloquent stylization of the face and the breasts, combine to create an impression of great monumentality and power.

Elephant. Bronze. China. Chou Period (11th-9th century B. C.). Length: 96 cm. Height: 64 cm. Guimet Museum.

This strange piece is, in fact, a *chueh*, a ritual vase with an opening in the animal's back. It comes from the impressive Camondo donation, bequeathed to the Louvre in 1908, the Asiatic items of which have since been brought together with those in the Guimet Museum. It is decorated with traditional *t'ao-t'ieh* designs, stylized in highly decorative strips. The expressive simplicity of the animal's stance perfectly suggests its enormous weight, uniting a sensitive naturalism with a plastic interpretation to achieve a balance and a perfection rarely seen.

26

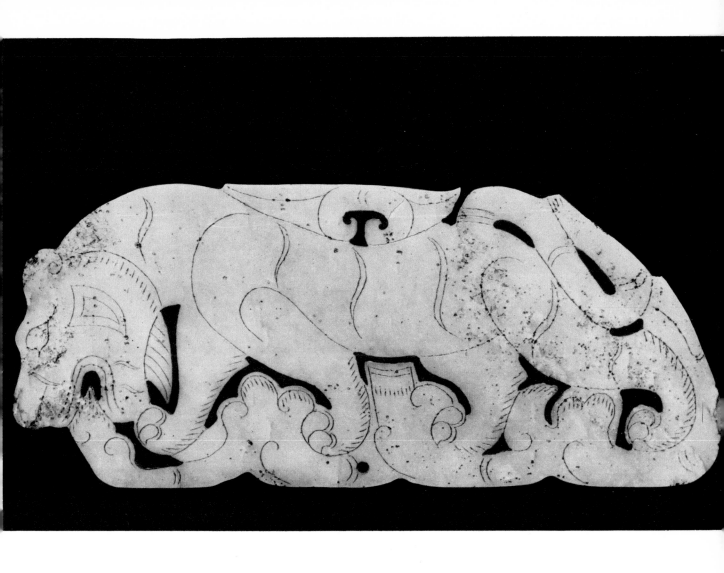

Tiger Jade. China. Han Period (3rd century B. C. - 3rd century A. D.). Length: 16 cm. Guimet Museum.

The motion of the white tiger, devouring a serpent, is brought out by means of a rhythmical animation resulting in a decorative effect. In this example, Chinese art joins up with a style of artistic expression widespread among the nomad peoples from Asia stretching as far west as Europe. Its origins are found in the bronzes of Luristan in Persia towards the 10th century B. C., while manifestations of it are also found in the Merovingian clasps in France. This art is characterized by its bold, stylized interpretation of animal life.

Pediment of the Temple of Bantéay-Srei. Stone. Khmer Art (Second half of 10th century A. D.). Height: 1.95 m. Width: 2.69 m. Guimet Museum.

This pediment over the door of the temple depicts an episode in the Ramayana legends: the two spirits, Sounda and Oupasunda, are competing for the possession of Tilottama. The sculpture combines a subtle evocation of the countryside, represented by the delicate foliage of trees, with a vibrant and harmonious treatment of the human form, of a nobility which approaches that of Greek statuary. One will note the skill with which the rhythmical attitudes and gestures have been fitted into the curves of the decorative framework.

Head of Buddha. Sandstone. Khmer Art (12th-13th century). Height: 25 cm. Guimet Museum.

This head of the Lokeçvara Buddha wears the typical smile of Khmer art, composed, meditative, pregnant with Buddhist wisdom, combined with a humanist tenderness which is deeply moving.

Dancing Apsaras. Stone. Khmer Art (end of 12th-beginning of 13th century A. D.). Height: 60 cm. Total length: 2.76 m. (detail). Guimet Museum.

Like the preceding piece, this work of sculpture belongs to the last period of great Khmer art, that of Bayon, the temple of Angkor, built about 1200. In all, the group contains nine apsaras, the mythical dancing girls whose traditions have been preserved up to the present day by the dancing girls of Cambodia. The perfect suppleness of their movements, charged with a controlled gaiety, has been conveyed in this relief sculpture with an ease and harmony which have both mystery and great originality.

Bodhisattva. Polychromed wood. Japan. Kamakura Period (13th century). Height: 85 cm. Guimet Museum.

Amida, the teacher-Buddha, raises his right hand in a ritual gesture. In its great medieval period, Japanese statuary, influenced by the art of China, is distinguished by a discretion and an elegance which give it great purity of style.

King Naga. Red sandstone. India. Mathura Period (1st-2nd century A.D.). Height: 1.16 m. Guimet Museum.

The figure depicted is a spirit of the waters, a rain-maker.

Spirit with Flowers. Stucco. Hadda, Afghanistan (3rd century A.D.). Height: 55 cm. Guimet Museum. ▶

There is a distant reminder of the Apollos of ancient Greece in this work of Greco-Buddhist sculpture.

The Lady and the Unicorn. Tapestry (end of 15th century). Height: 3.78 m. Width: 4.66 m. Cluny Museum.

Entitled *A mon seul désir*, this tapestry is one of the six pieces composing the most famous set of tapestries of medieval times. It comes from the Château of Boussac, where it caught the attention of George Sand, the first to celebrate its beauty, which she did in her novel, *Jeanne*, in 1844. Prosper Mérimée, as inspector of historical monuments, pointed out its importance too. Despite research, its meaning has remained obscure. In this tapestry the Lady is about to put on a necklace which she is taking from a jewel-box. She is flanked by heraldic animals, the lion and the unicorn, who are holding open the flaps of her tent. Domestic animals abound in the background of 'mille fleurs' on a red ground. Hieratic trees grow in the fields.

The Proffered Heart. Tapestry attributed to the Arras workshops (first third of 15th century). Height: 2.58 m. Width: 2.09 m. Cluny Museum. ▶

Tapestries were luxury articles in the 15th century, made for seigneurs. Their themes celebrated aristocratic life, as did the 'romans courtois', being often heroic and romantic in nature.

AUGUSTE RODIN *(Paris, 1840-Meudon, 1917): The Kiss. Marble. Height: 1.90 m. Rodin Museum.*

The most popular of Rodin's marbles, this was first conceived as part of his huge *Gate of Hell*, which was commissioned in 1880 but never completed. Inspired by Dante's *Divine Comedy*, the monument was designed to illustrate various episodes from the poem. This couple represents Paolo Malatesta and Francesca de Rimini. The present title was given to the work by a journalist.

VINCENT VAN GOGH *(Zundert, 1853 - Auvers-sur-Oise, 1890): Le Père Tanguy. Canvas. Height: 1.05 m. Width: 61 cm. Rodin Museum.* ▶

AUGUSTE RODIN: *The Prodigal Son. Marble, before 1894. Height: 1.40 m. Rodin Museum.*

Many different names have been given to this figure, first put on exhibition in 1894, among them: the *Child of the Century, Prayer, Invocation, The Supreme Call, The Prayer of the Abandoned Child.* It has also been interpreted as the figure of a dying warrior. Never has the desire to live been expressed in stone with the same force as here.

AUGUSTE RODIN: *The Thinker. Bronze, 1888. Height: 2 m. Rodin Museum.*

This photograph of Rodin's famous work, *Le Penseur*, shows it standing before the colonnade of the Pantheon, where it was sited between 1906 and 1922. Like *The Kiss* and *The Prodigal Son*, it originally formed part of the *Gate of Hell*, being placed in the very centre of the pediment. It was then known as *The Poet*, Rodin visualizing it as Dante contemplating the horrors of hell.

JEAN-HONORÉ FRAGONARD *(Grasse, 1732-Paris, 1806): The Model's Début. Oval canvas. Height: 1.50 m. Width: 63 cm. Jacquemart-André Museum.*

A young woman shows the painter the model's breasts, while he attempts, by raising her skirts with his stick, to examine her legs—the model shyly resisting. The stick in question is of the kind all painters used at the time to steady their hand, anxious as they were to attain the greatest precision. This delightful composition, with its fresh colours, its light, brisk touch and, above all, the tact, wit and grace with which the artist has handled a suggestive scene, typical of a licentious age, is regarded as one of Fragonard's masterpieces.

◀ JEAN-MARC NATTIER *(Paris, 1685-1766): The Marquise d'Antin. Canvas, 1738. Height: 1.18 m. Width: 96 cm. Jacquemart-André Museum.*

Put on exhibition at the Salon of 1738, this portrait of a young woman, married the preceding year to the Vice-Admiral of France, shows all the elegance and charm of the 18th century French aristocracy, which Nattier, the fashionable painter of the day, knew how to flatter, while preserving a subtle delicacy and truth which can move us even today.

FRANS HALS *(Antwerp, circa 1580-Haarlem, 1666): Portrait of a Man. Canvas. Height: 67 cm. Width: 59 cm. Jacquemart-André Museum.*

The Haarlem master devoted himself entirely to portrait painting, exalting the Dutch burghers in all their rough and energetic truth, men who had recently succeeded in their fight for freedom. Hals' final period, to which this portrait belongs, was characterized by his brusque and free brushwork. In the 19th century Frans Hals found a great admirer in Manet. His art, in fact, encouraged the Impressionists in their daring.

HARMENSZOON VAN RIJN, known as REMBRANDT *(Leyden, 1606-Amsterdam, 1669)*: *Christ at Emmaus.*
Paper on wood. Height: 37 cm. Width: 41 cm. Jacquemart-André Museum.

In the foreground a disciple kneels in the shadow thrown by the table, while another is struck
with fear and stupefaction at the apparition of Christ silhouetted against the light, whose source is
concealed behind his body. In the distance a woman is preparing a meal at the fire. This is the
oldest version of a theme Rembrandt treated several times over. After he had reached the age of
twenty-five, Rembrandt's genius began to flower, revealing itself in the originality and simplicity of
his *mise en scène*, the realism of his figures and the settings in which he placed them. One is struck
here by the rough simplicity of the one disciple, with the face of a beggar, contrasting with the
majesty of the figure of Christ, surrounded by supernatural light.

VITTORE CARPACCIO (*Venice, circa 1455-1525*): *The Ambassador of Hippolyta, Queen of the Amazons, to the Court of Theseus, King of Athens. Panel. Height: 1.02 m. Width: 1.45 m. Jacquemart-André Museum.*

◀ (*Detail*)

This episode in the history of Athens comes from the First Song of Boccaccio's *Teseide*. In it one recognizes the revived taste for antiquity. Yet the theme is still treated in the spirit of the romances of chivalry and the scene gives a faithful picture of the luxury of Venetian life at the close of the 15th century. A painter of pageants and historical scenes, Carpaccio was an adept at composing scenes containing many figures, in which nothing is conventional, in which each figure, each detail of the décor, is depicted with delicate precision and a genuine naïveté of great charm and poetry.

UCCELLO (*Florence, 1397-1477*): *St. George Slaying the Dragon. Tempera on panel. Height: 25 cm. Width: 90 cm. Jacquemart-André Museum.*
▶

The horseman is slaying the dragon which had issued from its cave and was about to devour the princess. In the distance one sees the town which has supplied the sacrificial victim. This episode symbolizes the 4th century martyr's victory over paganism. As was his custom, Uccello has painted the scene in the costumes of his own day, conferring on it a refined and aristocratic elegance. A great innovator and fascinated by perspective, he has succeeded in creating a sensation of space which is almost vertiginous.

45

Donatello *(Florence, circa 1386-1466):   The Martyrdom of St. Sebastian.   Bronze.   Height: 24 cm.   Width: 16 cm.   Jacquemart-André Museum.*

An angel has appeared to console the saint, tied to a pillar, as two archers prepare to shoot their arrows from close quarters.   The artist was no doubt constrained to group the figures in this unusual way in view of the space available to him, yet the result is most original, making the most of muscular tension and the supple lines of flowing robes.   The elegance of this great master of the Quattrocento, inspired by the art of antiquity, marks the triumphant début of the Renaissance.

FRANÇOIS-HUBERT DROUAIS *(Paris, 1727-1775): Small Boy Playing with a Cat. Oval canvas. Height: 58 cm. Width: 40 cm. Jacquemart-André Museum.*

Drouais le fils, as he signed himself, his father being a good portrait painter too, enjoyed great success at the court of Louis XVI. He made a speciality of painting children in the guise of gardeners, grape harvesters, savoyards. This portrait, more natural than those, has a charm which, though tending to the over-sweet, is nevertheless seductive.

JEAN-BAPTISTE PERRONNEAU *(Paris, 1715-Amsterdam, 1783): François Gillequin. Canvas. Height: 62 cm. Width: 52 cm. Jacquemart-André Museum.*

In this fine potrait in oils, Perronneau, better known for his pastels, displays his earnest and realist gifts as an observer, incapable of flattering his sitter. For this reason he was eclipsed at the French court by his brilliant rival, Quentin de la Tour. In recent times, however, interest in this artist has revived. He stands in the mainstream of French portrait painting.

REMBRANDT: *Rembrandt in Oriental Costume. Canvas, 1631. Height: 63 cm. Width: 56 cm. Petit Palais.*

This self-portrait, which has a companion piece in a portrait of the artist's sister, Lisbeth, shows the painter in the full flower of his youth, dressed like one of those rajahs the Dutch got to know so well from their sea trade. The poodle, unique in Rembrandt's portraits, has been painted with the same meticulous care as his master. The helmet and other objects in the background point to the beginnings of that passion for collecting which was to contribute to the artist's financial downfall.

Virgin and Child. Ivory. French art (beginning of 13th century). Height: 26 cm. Petit Palais.

In the keeping of the Abbaye d'Ourscamp, near Noyon, until 1789, this figure of the Virgin, carried in processions, is an excellent example of the work of French ivory-carvers at the time when their art was at its height. The purity of a style which still retains the quiet simplicity of the Romanesque period is united here with the flexibility, refined yet unceremonious, of early Gothic art.

ODILON REDON *(Bordeaux, 1840-Paris, 1916): Vase of Flowers. Pastel. Height: 65 cm. Petit Palais.*

Nowhere else is symbolist art so well represented as by the twenty-four works of Odilon Redon in the Petit Palais collection. He was the only authentic representative of this art with his profound feeling for colour and the subtle emotion with which he imbued his strange visions as well as the simple bouquets of flowers he painted, such as the one depicted here.

Candelabrum. St. Porchaire Faïence (16th century). Height: 31 cm. Petit Palais.

The pottery known as ' Henri II,' ' d'Oiron ' or ' St. Porchaire,' examples of which are highly rare, represents the highest degree of refinement attained by French ceramic art. Round the shaft are three putti, one of which bears the escutcheon of Henri II and Catherine de Médicis. The colours, yellow, brown and green, are of extreme delicacy.

J.-B. CARPEAUX *(Valenciennes, 1827-Courbevoie, 1875): The Three Graces. Terra cotta, 1872-1874. Height:*
77 cm. Petit Palais.　▶

GUSTAVE COURBET *(Ornans, 1819 - La Tour-de-Peilz, Switzerland, 1877):* The Young Ladies on the Shores of *the Seine. Canvas, 1856. Height: 1.73 m. Width: 2.06 m. Petit Palais.*

First shown at the Salon of 1857, *Les Demoiselles des bords de la Seine* disconcerted the public by their heaviness and air of tedium, which contrasted so sharply with the elegant insipidity then in fashion. The richness of the paint, the vigorous relief with which skin, clothing and vegetation have been painted here reveal Courbet's great, sensual love of life in all its aspects, the attribute by which he re-animated French painting. It will be found again in the work of the leading Impressionists, such as Renoir.

GUSTAVE COURBET: *P. J. Proudhon and his Children. Canvas. Height: 1.47 m. Width: 1.98 m. Petit Palais.*

A painting such as this is a testimony to friendship. Courbet associated himself with the philosopher in 1852, sharing his socialist ideals so wholeheartedly that he got himself exiled during his later years for the part he played in the Paris Commune. In this triple portrait he has raised the genre scene to the level of a high order of moral and symbolic painting, without any sacrifice of realism.

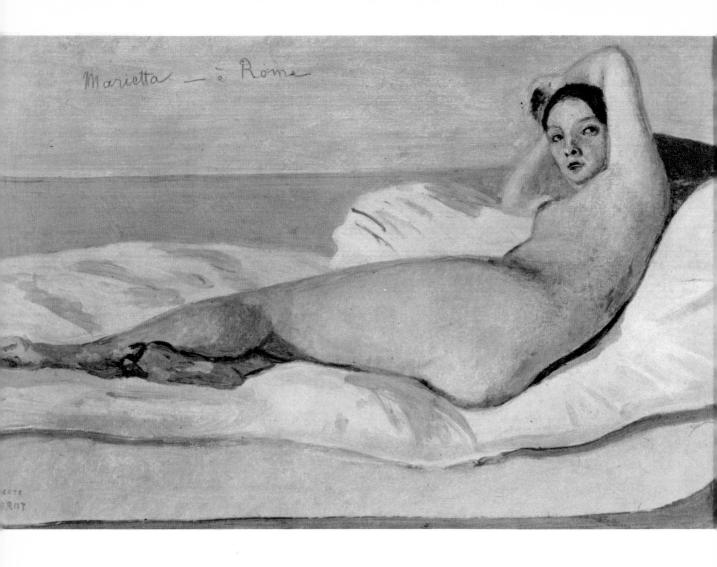

CAMILLE COROT *(Paris, 1796-1875)*: *Marietta. Canvas, 1843. Height: 29 cm. Width: 42 cm. Petit Palais.*

The inscription: *Marietta – à Rome,* has enabled us to date this work 1843, the year of Corot's second journey to Rome. A lifelike study, the work was never intended for exhibition and remained in the artist's studio until his death. The model's identity and her relationship to the artist have remained a matter of conjecture. The painting's main attraction is its harmony of tone and its direct, slightly naïve air. Corot, approaching fifty, had never before painted nudes. Afterwards, however, he created a fairly large number, more or less mythological in character and placed in a natural setting. Neglected in their own day, they are regarded very highly in ours.

HONORÉ DAUMIER *(Marseilles, 1808-Valmondois, 1879): The Connoisseur of Prints. Canvas. Height: 41 cm. Width: 33 cm. Petit Palais.*

Famous as a caricaturist, Daumier did not exhibit his canvases and was consequently almost unknown as a painter during his lifetime, despite the formidable talent so obvious in this work.

ÉDOUARD VUILLARD *(Cuisseaux, 1868-La Baule, 1940): Portrait of Bonnard. Canvas, 1935. Height: 1.15 m. Width: 1.46 m. Petit Palais.*

A friend of the painter Bonnard from the days of his youth, Vuillard, who founded the Nabi Group with him, painted this highly moving portrait of him towards the end of his life. He has succeeded in evoking the artist's solitude, confronted by his own work, setting him in an interior which Vuillard knew how to paint with all the refinement of the Dutch masters. It is as though Bonnard is experiencing here that sense of disquiet every artist has felt, the greatest included. The light adds mystery to this simple, touching scene.

ÉDOUARD MANET *(Paris, 1832-1883): Théodore Duret. Canvas, 1868. Height: 46 cm. Width: 35 cm. Petit Palais.* ▶

The art critic, Théodore Duret, who lived from 1838 to 1937, was a courageous supporter of the Impressionists, writing of them in various works published between 1878 and 1924. One of these was devoted to Manet and appeared in 1902, after the artist's death. Painted in 1868, this small portrait is rightly regarded as a masterpiece by virtue of the harmonious use of various shades of grey, relieved by the touch of yellow, and further by virtue of the freshness, elegance and vivacity of its execution.

PAUL CÉZANNE *(Aix, 1839-1906)*: *Ambroise Vollard. Canvas, 1899. Height: 1 m. Width: 82 cm. Petit Palais.*

The celebrated businessman, Vollard, who launched Cézanne on his career and so made a fortune, agreed to pose for this portrait one hundred and three times, perched on some barrels. When it was finished, Cézanne remarked: 'I'm reasonably pleased with the front of the shirt.'

HENRI FANTIN-LATOUR *(Grenoble, 1836-Buré, 1904)*: *The des Batignolles Studio. Canvas, 1870. Height: 2.04 m. Width: 2.70 m. Museum of Impressionism (Jeu de Paume)*.

Fantin-Latour was the first to show, in four canvases, the homage that was paid by their admirers to some of the artists of his time, an honour previously reserved for great political or military leaders. Exalting literature, music and painting, these four canvases have been reunited in the first room at the Museum of Impressionism. In this one, the hero is Manet, whom the young painters later to become known as the Impressionists acknowledged as their master. The artist is seen at his easel, painting the portrait of the sculptor, Zacharie Astruc. Behind him, from left to right, stand: the German painter, Scholderer, Renoir, Émile Zola, Edmond Maître, the critic, Bazille and Claude Monet. In this way Fantin-Latour brought together two groups of the artist's admirers, painters and writers. A new era was emerging—one in which the art critics were to play a major rôle in the defence of new art.

ÉDOUARD MANET: *The Balcony. Canvas, 1868-1869. Height: 1.69 m. Width: 1.25 m. Museum of Impressionism.* ▶

In the foreground sits Berthe Morisot, destined to become the artist's sister-in-law. Near her stands Jenny Claus, a musician, who was later to marry the painter, Prin., and behind the two ladies, a cigar in his hand, the landscape painter, Guillemet. A waiter can be seen bearing a tray in the left background. Inspired by Goya's *Manolas on the Balcony*, this magnificent canvas could please hardly anyone at the time and it therefore remained in Manet's studio. Caillebotte purchased it after his death for the small sum of 3,000 francs, offering it later with the rest of his collection to the former Luxembourg Museum.

63

Édouard Manet: *Portrait of Émile Zola.* *Canvas.* *Height: 1.45 m. Width: 1.14 m.* *Museum of Impressionism.*

In 1866 and 1867, Émile Zola came passionately to the defence of Manet in *l'Événement*, which he was obliged to leave as a result, and in the *Revue du XIXᵉ siècle*. In recognition of this, the artist painted this portrait of him, exhibited it at the Salon of 1868 and then made the author a present of it.

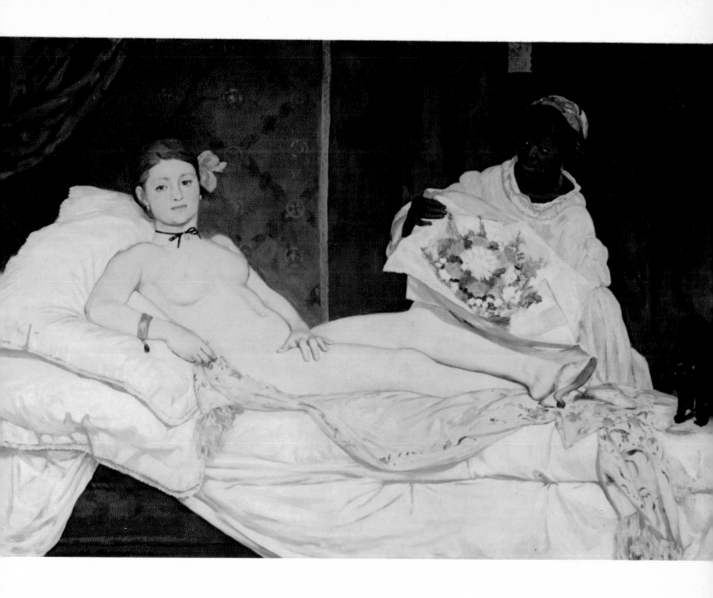

ÉDOUARD MANET: *Olympia. Canvas, 1863. Height: 1.30 m. Width: 1.90 m. Museum of Impressionism.*

The title *Olympia* has been taken from a poem, *La Fille des Iles,* by Zacharie Astruc, the friend and defender of Manet, who appears in Fantin-Latour's *l'Atelier des Batignolles* painting (p. 63). The model was Victorine Meurend, who also appears in *Le Déjeuner sur l'Herbe* and *The Fifer.* Accepted by the Salon of 1865, the painting provoked a great scandal and elicited the most furious invectives: 'This *Olympia* is a sort of female gorilla ... art which has descended to this level doesn't even deserve censure.' Baudelaire tried to cheer Manet, who was deeply affected, by saying: 'Do you think you have more genius than Chateaubriand and Wagner? They were ridiculed too but it didn't kill them.' Kept by Manet himself—he looked upon it as his masterpiece—this *Olympia* was offered to the state in 1890 and bought for 19,415 francs by means of a public subscription organized by Claude Monet. In 1907, efforts made by Monet and Georges Clemenceau, president of the Council, succeeded in getting the painting transferred to the Louvre and hung in the Salle des États, opposite Ingres' *l'Odalisque.*

◀ ÉDOUARD MANET: *Portrait of Zola (detail).*

67

ÉDOUARD MANET: *Le Déjeuner sur l'Herbe. Canvas, 1863. Height: 2.14 m. Width: 2.70 m. Museum of Impressionism.*

Refused by the selection committee of the Salon of 1863 and declared indecent by Napoleon III, this painting was exhibited at the famous Salon des Refusés that same year. The nude is Victorine Meurend, the model for the *Olympia* painting, while the men are Eugène Manet, brother of the painter, later the husband of Berthe Morisot, and the Dutch sculptor, Ferdinand Leenhoff, Manet's future brother-in-law. The colour effect in the foreground is rich, with the pale blue of the woman's dress, the yellow of her hat and basket and the red of the fruit. The source of the composition has been traced to an engraving of Marc Antony, based on a lost mythological painting by Raphael, in which all the figures are nude. It was the association in a modern painting of a naked woman among fully clothed men which provoked the scandal of which Zola wrote in *l'Oeuvre*. Nowadays we accept the boldness of this device, which can be found in Giorgione's *Concert Champêtre* also.

ÉDOUARD MANET: *Lola de Valence. Canvas, 1861-1862. Height: 1.23 m. Width: 92 cm. Museum of Impressionism.*

A group of Spanish ballet dancers, who had come to perform at the Hippodrome in Paris, agreed to pose for Manet in his friend, Stevens', studio near this theatre. The leading lady dancer attended one day only for the painter, who still made this dazzling portrait, posed against stage properties. The *chef d'oeuvre* of Manet's 'Spanish period', this canvas inspired Baudelaire, the artist's friend, to write the famous quatrain which ends with the words: ' ... le charme inattendu d'un bijou rose et noir.'

CLAUDE MONET *(Paris, 1840-Giverny, 1926): Regatta at Argenteuil. Canvas, circa 1872. Height: 48 cm. Width: 73 cm. Museum of Impressionism.*

Monet settled at Argenteuil from 1872 to 1878, often actually painting on the waters of the Seine, in a boat which served him as a floating studio. This enabled him to study the changing effect of the light on the water, the grass and trees and the sails, resulting in canvases of a marvellous freshness, the dawn, the triumphal chant, of Impressionism. The museum possesses six of them.

◀ CLAUDE MONET: *Women in the Garden. Canvas, 1866-1867. Height: 2.55 m. Width: 2.05 m. Museum of Impressionism.*

Done at Ville d'Avray, this canvas has the exceptional distinction of being the first compostion painted out-of-doors. Monet even had a ditch dug in the soil in order, with the aid of a pulley, to let the canvas down into it, while he was busy with the upper half. The model for all four figures was Camille, later the artist's wife. The extreme freshness of tone has been achieved by the lightness with which the colour has been treated, making a break with the large flat surfaces of colour in the Courbet manner which Monet was using only a year before. Thus this painting really does mark a revolution in painting. Painted for Bazille, who bought it for 2,500 francs, paying 50 francs each month, the canvas passed to Renoir, who returned it to Monet at the end of a quarrel. Monet sold it to the state in 1921 for 200,000 francs. It became part of the Louvre's collection in 1929.

CLAUDE MONET: *St.-Lazare Station. Canvas, 1877. Height: 75 cm. Width: 1 m. Museum of Impressionism.*

The seven canvases which Claude Monet devoted to the St.-Lazare railway station in Paris formed the first of a series which he was later to devote to such divergent themes as hay-ricks, poplars, cathedrals, nymphs. Only Turner (in 1844) had preceded Monet in the painting of this modern theme, in which, amid smoke, the light is all a-quiver. The impressionist painter has created a singular and intense poetry of colour out of it, turning the smoke from the locomotive into the purest of blues.

CLAUDE MONET: *The Cathedral of Rouen, in full sunlight. Canvas, 1894. Height: 1.07 m. Width: 73 cm. Museum of Impressionism.* ▶

In February 1892, Monet settled in a room in Rouen, at 81, rue du Grand-Pont, facing the cathedral. There he painted twenty compositions at different hours of the day, five of which have been brought together in a room at the Museum of Impressionism. He worked on the series for two years. 'The more I do', he wrote, 'the harder I find it to convey what I feel.'

ALFRED SISLEY *(Paris, 1839 - Moret-sur-Loing, 1899): The Flood at Port-Marly. Canvas, 1876. Height: 60 cm. Width 81 cm. Museum of Impressionism.*

The theme of the flood, with its vast expanses of water, was particularly attractive to the impressionist painters. Sisley was happiest at putting it to good effect, transforming the tragic aspect of the subject into a symphony of lucent, trembling touches. Neither did he fail to portray the beauty of ordinary houses which remind us of Utrillo's, who proclaimed himself to be Sisley's disciple. The artist painted five canvases in 1876, while at Port-Marly. Unfortunate all his life, Sisley was never able to obtain more than a few hundred francs for his paintings, whilst this particular example was bought, only a few months after his death, for as much as 45,150 francs, by the Comte Camondo, who bequeathed it to the Louvre in 1908.

CAMILLE PISSARRO *(Saint Thomas, Danish Antilles, 1830 - Paris, 1903):* *The Red Roofs.* *Canvas, 1877.*
Height: 53 cm. Width: 53 cm. Museum of Impressionism.

Less attracted by river landscapes than were Monet and Sisley, Pissarro chose for his abode the
quiet countryside round Pontoise, where he stayed from 1872 to 1884. Cézanne, Guillaumin and
Gauguin were attracted by it too. In this canvas, painted in the winter, we see sturdy farm buildings
through the leafless trees, sheltered in a hollow of the fields. The rich and heavy texture of the paint
and the close structure of the various masses suggest the influence of the painter's friend, Cézanne,
who worked together with him in this region between 1872 and 1874. A comparison with Cézanne's
painting, *The Hanged Man's House,* on page 84, is telling.

AUGUSTE RENOIR *(Limoges, 1841-Cagnes, 1919)*: *The Inn of Le Moulin de la Galette. Canvas, 1876. Height: 1.31 m. Width: 1.75 m. Museum of Impressionism.*

This country pub, where artists and young girls loved to come to dance, has been transfigured by the artist into a poem of youthful happiness. It was done entirely on the spot according to Georges Rivière, who is one of the figures sitting at the table on the right. The other main figures were models and friends of Renoir, including two other fairly well-known painters, Gervex and Goeneutte. At a later date, Renoir stated that the lacquers mixed with white have faded out and that the painting has changed as a result, the blue now dominating, which it did not originally.

◀ AUGUSTE RENOIR: *Girl Reading. Canvas, circa 1875-1876. Height: 47 cm. Width: 38 cm. Museum of Impressionism.*

Seated against the light at a window, the young girl is doubtlessly lit by a lamp as well. The subject matter, which is in the spirit of the 18th century painters Renoir so greatly admired, has become entirely modern, nevertheless, as a result of long, delicate and rapid strokes of the brush, the extremely subtle play of light and Renoir's very special sense of femininity.

EDGAR DEGAS *(Paris, 1834-1917): Absinth. Canvas, 1876. Height: 92 cm. Width: 68 cm. Museum of Impressionism.*

The models for this painting were not, as it might seem, miserable social outcasts, but the engraver, Marcellin Desboutins, and the actress, Ellen Andrée, who agreed to come along to the Café de la Nouvelle Athènes and pose for Degas in these clothes and attitudes.

◄ EDGAR DEGAS: *The Ballet School at the Opera House in the rue Le Peletier. Canvas, 1872. Height: 32 cm. Width: 46 cm. Museum of Impressionism.*

EDGAR DEGAS: *Ballerina on Stage. Pastel, circa 1878. Height: 58 cm. Width: 24 cm. Museum of Impressionism.*

Differing from his impressionist friends, being uninterested in nature, Degas was passionately interested in subjects drawn from modern life and particularly from the theatre. An *habitué* of the Paris Opera, a familiar face behind the scenes, he made study upon study of movement, his prodigious gifts as a draughtsman enabling him to capture the dancers' most fleeting attitudes. He stylizes them in the artificial glare of the footlights, painting the most refined of compositions and arranging his material in the most original and unexpected ways on the canvas.

VINCENT VAN GOGH. *(Zundert, 1853 - Auvers-sur-Oise, 1890). The Artist's Room at Arles. Canvas, 1889. Height: 56 cm. Width: 74 cm. Museum of Impressionism.*

This canvas is a replica which Van Gogh made at the hospital of Saint Rémy of the one he had done the year before in the bedroom at Arles, furnished by himself. He commented on the painting as follows: ' It's my bedroom — just that. Here everything depends on the colour. By making the objects seem grander due to its simplifying effect, it is meant to suggest the general idea of rest or sleep.'

VINCENT VAN GOGH: *The Church at Auvers. Canvas, 1890. Height: 94 cm. Width: 74 cm. Museum of Impressionism.*
▶

Originating from Dr. Gachet's collection and never exhibited before arriving at the museum in 1951, this canvas is more than a landscape. It is about the painter's final tragedy, too, and was painted a few weeks before his suicide. The violence of the colours and the tension of the lines which surround and overwhelm the calm of this medieval edifice betray the artist's terrible agony of mind as he sensed that he had come to the end of his tortured career. This work and that of his gay little bedroom opposite represent the two poles of Van Gogh's destiny.

PAUL CÉZANNE *(Aix, 1839-1906): The Hanged Man's House. Canvas, 1873. Height: 55 cm. Width: 66 cm. Museum of Impressionism.*

The loveliest of the paintings Cézanne did at Auvers-sur-Oise bears a tragic title, which almost seems to predict the drama that was to take place in the same village seventeen years later, when Van Gogh committed suicide there. Yet the name has no foundation, for in fact no one hanged himself in the house. Nevertheless, the atmosphere of the painting is grave and slightly sinister.

PAUL GAUGUIN *(Paris, 1848-Atuana, 1903): The White Horse. Canvas, 1898. Height: 1.41 m. Width: 91 cm. Museum of Impressionism.* ▶

This canvas was painted during Gauguin's second stay on Tahiti.

Henri Rousseau, *known as* Le Douanier Rousseau *(Laval, 1844-Paris, 1910): War. Canvas, 1894. Height: 1.13 m. Width: 1.93 m. Museum of Impressionism.*

A strange woman with long black hair, clothed in a short, frayed white dress and brandishing a sword in one hand, a smoking torch in the other, rides astride a monstrous black courser. The other title the painting bears — *The Ride of Discord* — indicates the symbolism of this figure, charging over the naked bodies of the dying as they are torn at by crows. Exhibited at the Salon des Indé-pendants in 1894, the picture formed the subject of a lithograph which Rousseau did by order of Remy de Gourmont, who published it in *l'Imagier*. From this date onwards, the painter affirmed the complete originality of his style, which may be compared with that of the primitives by reason of its linear clarity, the exquisite freshness of the colours, including some beautiful blacks, which Degas appreciated too, but, above all, by reason of the direct and unheard of intensity of this naïveté, which was later to start a school.

◀ Georges Seurat *(Paris, 1859-1891): Model, front view. Wood, 1887. Height: 26 cm. Width: 17 cm. Museum of Impressionism.*

Seurat made several small sketches for the great painting known as *les Poseuses*, today in the keeping of the Barnes Foundation in the U.S.A. Three of these stetches are in the Museum of Impressionism. Adopting the divisionist technique he had himself invented, he painted them with tiny dots arranged in connected layers, like the stitches in cloth, and extending as far as the border. The extreme purity of the drawing gives this very precise work great style and grace.

MAURICE DENIS *(Granville, 1870-Paris, 1943): Homage to Cézanne. Canvas, 1900. Height: 1.80 m. Width: 2.40 m. National Museum of Modern Art.*

Following Fantin-Latour's example (where Delacroix and Manet had been concerned), Maurice Denis sought to assemble Paul Cézanne's admirers in a collective portrait. Grouped round a canvas by the master of Aix stand, from left to right: Odilon Redon, Vuillard, Mellerio, the critic, Vollard, the merchant in whose boutique the reunion took place, Maurice Denis himself, Sérusier, who is busy giving a talk, Ranson, K. X. Roussel, Bonnard, smoking a cigarette, and Mme. Maurice Denis. In other words: these are the members of the Nabi movement.

◄ AMEDEO MODIGLIANI *(Livorno, 1884-Paris, 1920): Woman with a Fan. Canvas, 1919. Height: 1 m. Width: 65 cm. Municipal Museum of Modern Art.*

The grace of this elongated figure introduced into modern art an interest in the arabesque which is related to the art of the 15th century Italian primitives, although the nostalgic expression on the sitter's face is a reflection of the personal distress of the *artiste maudit* that Modigliani was.

PIERRE BONNARD *(Fontenay-aux-Roses, 1867-Le Cannet, 1947): Winter Day. Canvas, circa 1905. Height: 49 cm. Width: 60 cm. National Museum of Modern Art.*

Painted in Bonnard's studio in the rue de Douai, this canvas is a good example of the intimate character of the works of the Nabi group, who were content to evoke the quiet, orderly life of the everyday occupations in the bourgeois home. In this way they revived, with happy results, the *genre* painting of the old Dutch masters.

PIERRE BONNARD: *Woman at her Toilet. Canvas, circa 1922. Height: 1.20 m. Width: 80 cm. National Museum of Modern Art.* ▶

As the years passed, Bonnard's talent turned towards fuller forms and a refined analysis of limpid and iridescent colours. One of his themes became studies of nudes in the bathroom or bath-tub; works in which he demonstrated a subtle mastery of decomposed light.

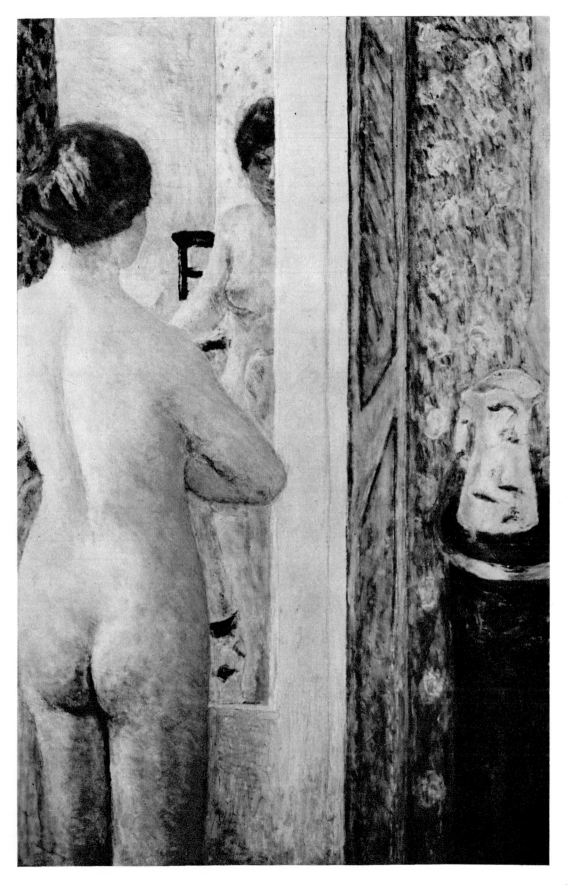

ÉDOUARD VUILLARD (*Cuiseaux, 1868-La Baule, 1940*): *Breakfast. Oil on carboard, circa 1900. Height: 57 cm. Width: 60 cm. National Museum of Modern Art.*

The artist's mother, the sitter for this painting, inspired some of his most expressive canvases. In this one we must especially admire the care with which Vuillard has conveyed both the natural attitude of the sitter and the details of this bourgeois interior, in which each section of the décor seems to possess a life of its own. The perfect unity and atmosphere of the whole is due to the artist's treatment of the light.

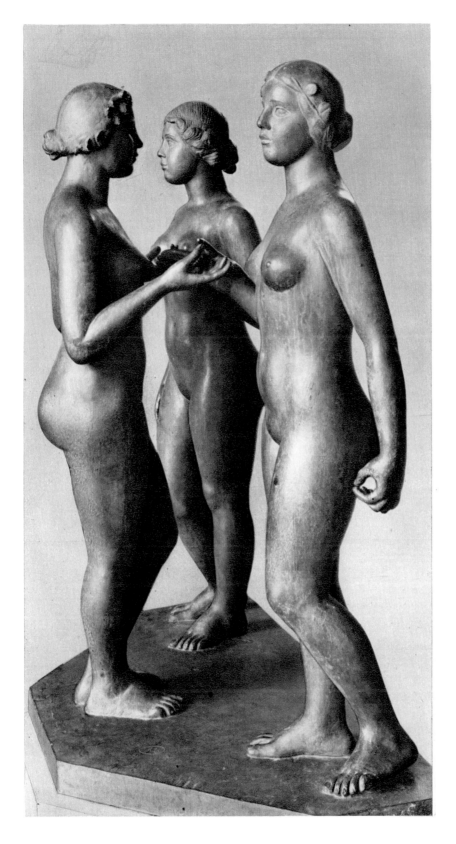

ARISTIDE MAILLOL *(Banyuls-sur-Mer, 1861 - Perpignan, 1944)*: *The Three Nymphs. Lead, 1936-1938. Height: 1.60 m. National Museum of Modern Art.*

GEORGES ROUAULT *(Paris, 1871-1958)*: *The Apprentice Workman. Canvas, circa 1925. Height: 68 cm. National Museum of Modern Art.*

This famous painting is in fact a self-portrait to which Rouault gave this title out of humility, thus conferring a general and classical significance on the work.

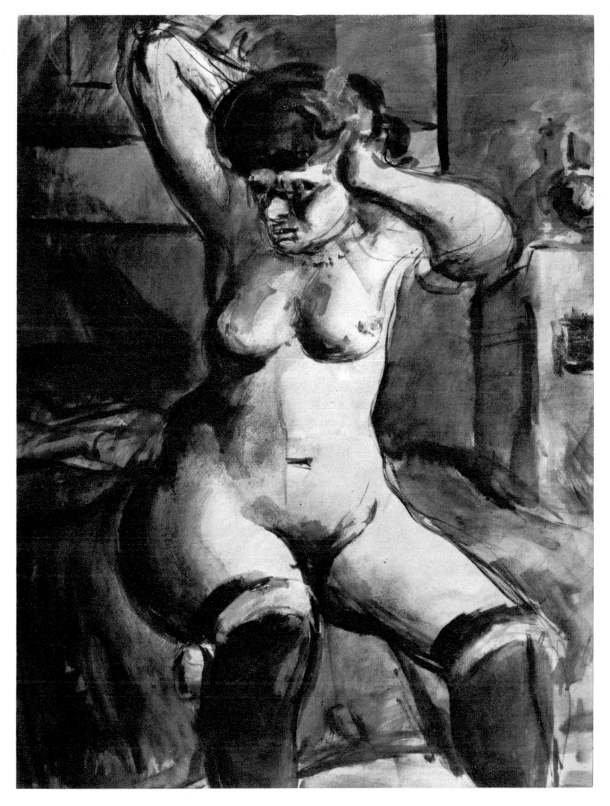

GEORGES ROUAULT: *Girl. Gouache, aquarelle and pastel, 1906. Height: 71 cm. Width: 55 cm. Municipal Museum of Modern Art.*

Dr. Girardin bequeathed ninety works of Rouault to the City of Paris, including this important gouache in his first manner. The painter has conferred a dramatic grandeur on a plebeian subject.

SUSANNE VALADON *(Bessines-sur-Gartempe, 1867 - Paris, 1938). The Blue Room. Canvas, 1923. Height: 91 cm. Width: 1.16 m. National Museum of Modern Art.*

A former model of Renoir, Puvis de Chavannes, Toulouse-Lautrec and Degas, Susanne Valadon received some advice on drawing from the last-named. Coming late to painting, she revealed the robust talent of the self-taught painter, characterized by energetic draughtsmanship, bold outlines, crude and brilliant colours and an aggressive propensity for painting popular subjects. The mother of Maurice Utrillo, she directed his interest to painting in order to tear him away from his vice of drinking.

MAURICE UTRILLO *(Paris, 1883-Dax, 1955): Rue Sainte-Rustique à Montmartre. Canvas, 1926. Height: 82 cm. Width: 60 cm. National Museum of Modern Art.* ▶

The streets of Montmartre, the suburbs and churches were the exclusive subjects of this *artiste maudit.* He had the gift of instilling into them a nostalgic lyricism and an expressive power which made him, before 1915, a very great painter.

96

RAOUL DUFY *(Le Havre, 1877 - Forcalquier, 1953)*: *The Paddock at Deauville. Canvas, circa 1930. Height: 54 cm. Width: 1.30 m. National Museum of Modern Art.*

The painting of modern life commended by Baudelaire has not interested 20th century artists as much as pure, aesthetic experience. Happily, this is not the case with Raoul Dufy. After having taken part in the Fauves movement and created his own original style, composed of colourful, nimble signs, he decided to apply this to evoke the most diverse contemporary spectacles: official receptions, large concerts, farm machinery at work, and shipping. One of his favourite subjects was the races. In *The Paddock at Deauville* he sought to show us a typical scene of the elegant life of his time. The small red buildings strike a gay contrast with the white railings and the summer greenery a-quiver

under a clear blue sky. The work is expansive in the manner of Far Eastern painting, inviting us to walk under the trees, coming across unexpected views at every turn, and to marvel with the artist at so many charming details. The horses and their jockeys have been conveyed by elliptical strokes superimposed on spots of pure colour. They introduce lively notes, assimilated in a joyous concert of colours in which everything is grace and *joie de vivre* 'sans rien qui pèse ou qui pose,' as Verlaine has put it. In Dufy's work the natural is joined with a simplicity which comes close to naïveté—but in appearance only, for this work has been executed with great virtuosity.

OTHON FRIESZ (*Le Havre, 1879-Paris, 1949*): *Portrait of Fernand Fleuret. Canvas, 1907. Height: 76 cm. Width: 60 cm. National Museum of Modern Art.*

Poet, novelist, art critic, Fernand Fleuret was haunted by insanity. His disquiet and instability are apparent in this painting, with its curiously plunging perspective, emphasizing the enormous skull. The colours clash violently, stressing the melancholy black of the anxious sitter.

KEES VAN DONGEN *(Delfshaven, The Netherlands, 1877): Portrait of the Artist as Neptune. Canvas, 1922. Height: 1.70 m. Width: 1.20 m. National Museum of Modern Art.*

A souvenir of a fancy-dress ball given by the painter in his studio in the rue Juliette Lambert, this self-portrait conjures up the immediate post-war years, in the 'twenties, when Van Dongen, the painter of the day, was turning out countless numbers of these brilliant, often savage portraits.

MAURICE DE VLAMINCK *(Paris, 1876 - Rueil-la-Gadelière, 1958): Landscape with Red Trees. Canvas, 1906 Height: 65 cm. Width: 81 cm. National Museum of Modern Art.*

Overwhelmed by an exhibition of Van Gogh's work which he visited in 1901, together with his friend, Derain, Vlaminck decided to use pure colours to express their most direct, their most powerful private feelings. This led to Fauvism, of which this landscape is a brilliant example, with its massive forms, thickly outlined, and its colours, exploding 'like cartridges full of dynamite'.

ANDRÉ DERAIN *(Chatou, 1880-Chambourcy, 1954): The Blonde. Canvas, 1928. Height: 37 cm. Width: 32 cm. National Museum of Modern Art.* ▶

After having been one of Fauvism's most ardent champions, Derain, an artist of great culture, frequent visitor to the museums, decided to leave games with pure colour behind him and return to 'le grand style,' founded on solid draughtsmanship. This beautiful study of the back of a woman's head and neck demonstrates the balance and the sculptural power which he achieved in his best canvases.

HENRI MATISSE *(Le Cateau, 1869-Cimiez, 1954)*: *The Sideboard. Canvas, 1928. Height: 83 cm. Width: 1.03 m. National Museum of Modern Art.*

Matisse adopted several different styles of painting in succession. Intelligent, restless, the artist was always searching for greater purity of line and colour. This painting represents a particularly happy moment of equilibrium in his œuvre, the objects depicted having retained their weight and relief, although adapted to a decided pattern and lively justapositions of colour.

HENRI MATISSE: *The Painter and His Model. Canvas, 1917. Height: 1.47 m. Width: 97 cm. National Museum of Modern Art.*

▶

Painted in his studio along the Quai St.-Michel, this work belongs to an austere period in Matisse's career. The simplified forms and the sober and severe colours show a certain Cubist influence. Nevertheless, the baroque mirror, the view of la Cité through the window, and, above all, the luminous atmosphere, reminiscent of Baudelaire, give the canvas a nostalgic grandeur, rare in Matisse's work.

ALBERT MARQUET (*Bordeaux, 1875-Paris, 1947*). *Rotterdam. Canvas, 1914. Height: 65 cm. Width: 61 cm. National Museum of Modern Art.*

Marquet has the purety of colour of the Fauves, while having rejected their gratuitous use of it. Becoming the painter of the quaysides and ports of all Europe, he was gifted at expressing the glitter of the water, the solidity of matter, the contrast between the elements and human activity, with an ease and simplicity which are immediately convincing.

MARC CHAGALL (*Vitebsk, 1887*): *Double Portrait with a Glass of Wine. Canvas, 1917. Height: 2.33 m. Width: 1.36 m. National Museum of Modern Art.* ▶

With his home town of Vitebsk in the background and perched on the shoulders of his wife as she wades through the waters of the river, the painter raises his glass to toast the anniversary of their marriage, while an angel floats above his head. In this extraordinary fantasy one witnesses the happy and vivifying encounter between Slav folklore, Jewish humour and the plastic qualities, the precision of form and brilliant colours of the École de Paris.

PABLO PICASSO *(Malaga, 1881): The Enamel Saucepan. Canvas, 1945. Height: 82 cm. Width: 1.06 m. National Museum of Modern Art.*

A white jug, a lighted candle in a brass candlestick, a blue enamel saucepan on a table of brown wood—these were sufficient for Picasso to be able to create a still life of magical charm. The date on the back of the frame, February 17, 1945, suggests that he needed only one day to paint this large canvas. His talent is characterized by rapidity and decision. The brilliance of the colours, the very heavy black outlines, the flattened surfaces are all crucial features of his style in this period.

PABLO PICASSO: *Seated Nude. Oil on cardboard, 1905. Height: 1.06 m. Width: 71 cm. National Museum of Modern Art.*

▶

Many consider Picasso's blue period, from 1903 to 1905, to be his best. His pure and classic draughtsmanship, the restraint of the delicate shades of colour, the nostalgic, sorrowful and proud expression of the figures vie with each other to confer on the works he painted at this time a poignant and unforgettable expressiveness. Although unfinished, this work is one of the best examples.

ANDRÉ DUNOYER DE SEGONZAC *(Boussy-Saint-Antoine, 1884): The de l'Aire Farm at St. Tropez. Canvas, 1925. Height: 35 cm. Width: 80 cm. National Museum of Modern Art.*

A quiet farmhouse, a few majestic trees, a spot of blue water are all the ingredients Dunoyer de Segonzac required to recreate the atmosphere of the French countryside in summer, whether in the Ile-de-France or, as here, in Provence. Saint-Tropez, where the artist has lived since 1925, has been a source of inspiration to him when painting both oils and aquarelles, in which he possesses supreme mastery ... an inspiration for powerful visions in which the haughty architecture of the mountains is united with the immense calm of the sea. Segonzac's art, firmly established in the tradition of French realism, joins a robust simplicity to an aristocratic refinement to arrive at a synthesis of classical grandeur.

MARCEL GROMAIRE *(Noyelles-sur-Sambre, 1892): Man Sharpening Scythe. Canvas, 1924. Height: 1 m. Width: 80 cm. Municipal Museum of Modern Art.* ▶

This painting is a good example of the way in which during his first period Gromaire transformed subjects taken from the life of the working class into simplified structures of great severity and monumentality.

ROGER DE LA FRESNAYE *(Le Mans, 1885-Grasse, 1925): The Cuirassier. Canvas, 1910. Height: 1.80 m. Width: 1.80 m. National Museum of Modern Art.*

Holding a horse by the bridle turned to the left behind him, the cuirassier is turned to face us. Soldiers can be seen passing, brandishing a flag, in the background. Here La Fresnaye is applying Cubism to the portrayal of movement, like the Italian Futurists. At the same time he uses this style to express a military theme, similar to those by Géricault. An energetic dynamism is manifest in this large painting, full of tension and measured power. War, heralded in this canvas of the year 1910, was to ruin la Fresnaye's health and thwart his great ambition: to create a modern classicism.

JACQUES VILLON *(Damville, 1875-Puteaux, 1963): The Adventure. Canvas, 1935. Height: 1.63 m. Width: 1.15 m. National Museum of Modern Art.*

Villon called himself an 'impressionist cubist.' He sought to add to purely plastic preoccupations the portrayal of light and movement, also the portrayal of indoor life. This desire is apparent in the figure depicted here, the geometrical surfaces concealing a sensitive and penetrating vision of the adventure of reading a book.

GEORGES BRAQUE *(Argenteuil, 1882-Varangeville, 1963): The Duet. Canvas, 1937. Height: 1.30 m. Width: 1.60 m. National Museum of Modern Art.*

One woman is seated at the piano in a room while the other is singing, holding in her hand a piece of music bearing the name of Debussy. The lucid composition is strongly stylized in the Cubist tradition, the figures being represented from the front and in profile at one and the same time and the drawing superimposed on patches of colour. The colours are lively, yellow, pink and orange on the left side, while in the shadows on the right greens and dark browns dominate.

ANDRÉ BAUCHANT *(Chateau-Renault, 1873-Montoire, 1958): Louis XI Having Mulberry Trees Planted Near Tours. Canvas, 1943. Height: 1.90 m. Width: 1.02 m. National Museum of Modern Art.* ▶

Bauchant, a nurseryman, is the only self-taught artist to have painted large mythological and historical works. His fresh, delicate colours and the spontaneity of his imagination make him a genuine primitive.

114

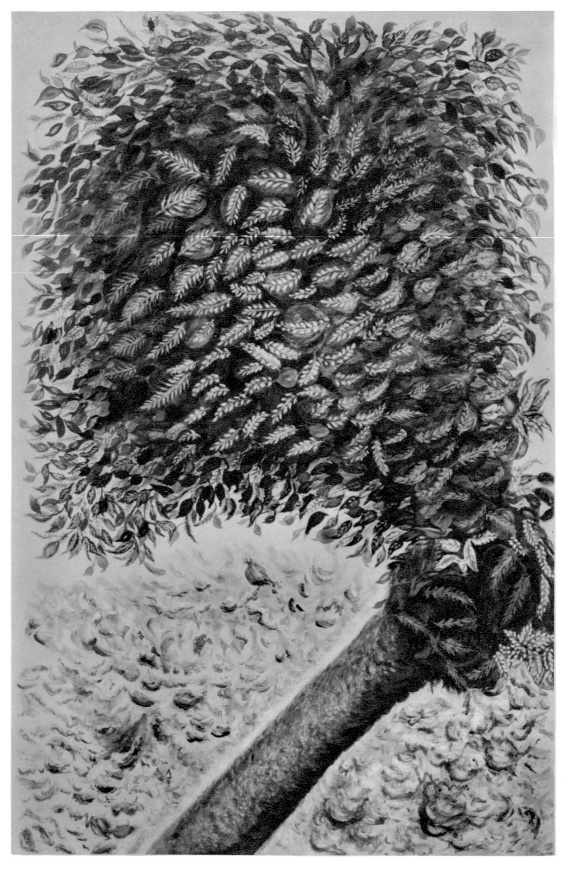

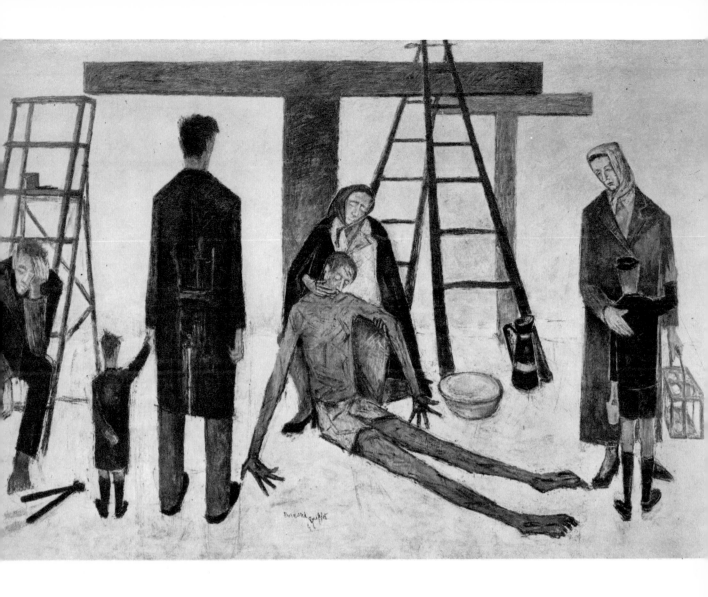

BERNARD BUFFET *(Paris, 1928): Pietà. Canvas, 1946. Height: 1.72 m. Width: 2.55 m. National Museum of Modern Art.*

This vast painting is the work of a young man of eighteen, who, two years later, was to win the Prix de la Critique and become the most startling discovery of the immediate post-war years. The artist's style is already wholly determined by the straight, implacable lines of the drawing, the monumental sobriety of the composition, the originality displayed in transforming this religious scene into a modern, working-class scene and, above all, by the petrified, transfixed manner in which suffering and drama are here depicted.

◀ SÉRAPHINE LOUIS (known as SÉRAPHINE DE SENLIS) *(Arsy, Oise, 1864 - Clermont, 1934): The Red Tree. Canvas, circa 1927-1928. Height: 1.93 m. Width: 1.30 m. National Museum of Modern Art.*

At the end of a miserable existence as a charwoman in Senlis, Séraphine, self-taught and discovered by the critic Wilhelm Uhde in 1912, painted a number of fantastic canvases based on plants and trees. They put her in the first rank of 20th century naïve painters.

NICOLAS DE STAËL *(St. Petersburg, 1914-Antibes, 1955): The Roofs. Canvas, 1952. Height: 2 m. Width: 1.50 m. National Museum of Modern Art.*

From 1944 to 1949, Nicolas de Staël was a determined exponent of abstract painting. But he was soon to attempt to go beyond abstraction in search of a simplified and more precise figuration. *The Roofs* marks one stage in this evolution. The subject is fairly recognizable, yet the elements drawn from reality continue to be schematic: elementary geometrical shapes, of delicate coloured tones.

HUBERT ROBERT *(Paris, 1733-1808): The Demolition of the Bastille. Canvas, 1789. Height: 77 cm.
Width: 1.14 m. Carnavalet Museum.*

Exhibited at the Salon of 1789, this canvas is of exceptional historical interest. The splendid
medieval fortress, which had become the symbol of a detested despotic régime to the French, rises
up in all its majesty at the very moment that it is being taken by assault. Here Hubert Robert,
painter of ancient ruins, had found a modern subject which allowed his visionary gifts full play in
a dramatic atmosphere that clearly announces the arrival of Romanticism.

PIERRE MIGNARD *(Troyes, 1612 - Paris, 1695): Madame de Sévigné. Canvas. Height: 81 cm. Width: 65 cm. Carnavalet Museum.*

Madame de Sévigné, the most celebrated of the wealthy occupiers of the Carnavalet mansion, lived there from 1677 to 1696. One of the rooms in the museum contains numerous souvenirs of this great lady, the most refined of the ' précieuses.' This portrait, attributed by some art critics to Claude Lefebvre, is a fine evocation of the delicate beauty, discreet elegance, and, above all, of the witty but at the same time deeply sensitive expression of this illustrious letter-writer.

ANTOINE COYSEVOX *(Lyons, 1640-Paris, 1720): Louis XIV. Bronze. Height: 2.50 m. Carnavalet Museum.*

Commissioned in 1687 and first put on display in 1689, this statue, which once stood before the Hôtel de Ville in Paris, can now be found in the court-yard of the Carnavalet Museum. Here the most celebrated sculptor of the Grand Siècle, who has left so many monuments in French churches and at Versailles, has created a haughty figure of the Roi-Soleil in his prime, dressed, in the manner of the day, in Roman costume, which seemed nobler, being associated with the heroes of Antiquity.

PHILIBERT LOUIS DEBUCOURT *(Paris, 1755-Belleville, 1832)*: *Fête at Les Halles in 1782. Canvas. Height: 90 cm. Width: 1.17 m. Carnavalet Museum.*

Although best known as an engraver, Debucourt left a few paintings too, of which this one is the most remarkable. It is of historical interest in that it shows us the popular festivities on January 21 1782, on the occasion of the birth of the Dauphin. It also shows us the exact appearance of Les Halles at the time, just before they were radically altered. The old pillory, reconstructed in the 16th century, can be seen, the des Halles Fountain of 1605, the market halls known as la Marée and la Saline (of timber and plaster), which were totally destroyed at the end of the 18th century. The painting, in the Flemish style much in fashion at the time, shows the violin orchestra on the left and the buffet, with barrels, on the right, while the crowd is dancing and enjoying itself in the middle.

◄ CARMONTELLE *(Paris, 1717-1806)*: *Mozart with his father and sister. Aquarelle and gouache. Height: 33 cm. Width: 20 cm. Carnavalet Museum.*

The trio depicted here consists of the young Mozart, dressed in blue at the clavecimbel, his father, Leopold, dressed in pink, and Nannerl, his sister, singing.

CAMILLE COROT *(Paris, 1796-1875): The Seine at the Quai des Orfèvres. Canvas, 1833. Height: 46 cm. Width: 63 cm. Carnavalet Museum.*

Although Corot was born in Paris, where his mother kept a dress shop on the corner of the rue du Pont-Royal, he rarely painted in the capital. This canvas, the most important one he has left us of Paris, was done after his first visit to trip to Italy, from 1825 to 1828. Apart from its documentary interest, it is an example of the artist's first manner. It has the skill of composition, the fineness of tone, the precise depiction of urban architecture, and, above all, the great sensitivity to atmosphere which was Corot's special contribution to French painting.

MONSÙ DESIDERIO *(Naples, beginning of the 17th century): Fantastic Landscape. Canvas. Height: 96 cm. Width: 74 cm. Museum of Decorative Arts.*

The name Monsù Desiderio conceals the identity of two painters, François Nomé and Didier Barra, who came from Metz and who specialized in painting historical and mythological scenes.

Small Drawing-room decorated with panels in the style of Oudry (circa 1750).   Museum of Decorative Arts.

This exquisite collection of painted woodwork comes from a house at No. 9 Place Vendôme. The paintings, in the manner of Jean-Baptiste Oudry (1686-1755), the famous painter of animals, represent various subjects from the fables of La Fontaine, favourite subjects in all the arts at the time, in tapestry, ceramics and cabinet-making.   In the tall panel one recognizes *The Fox and the Crow*, most famous of them all.

JEAN BERAIN *(1639-1711): Earthenware Dish. Moustiers, beginning of 18th century. Height: 38 cm. Width: 58 cm. Museum of Decorative Arts.*

An architect, draughtsman and engraver, Berain was the great interior decorator of the last years of Louis XIV's reign, famous for his 'grotesque' tapestries made at Beauvais, his costumes and *décors* for the theatre, and his Boulle furniture. This dish, with its arch enclosing an Apollo with three nymphs bathing, has been conceived as though for stage *décor*, or for some grove at Versailles. The fine earthenware of Moustiers began to appear about 1660 and lasted almost until the end of the 18th century. There were five periods, this dish belonging to the second, the Berain period, a blue-and-white period of a restrained elegance.

FRANÇOIS DESPORTES *(Champigneulles, circa 1661-Paris, 1743): The Silver Soup Tureen. Canvas. Height: 58 cm. Width: 72 cm. Museum of Decorative Arts.*

This unfinished canvas from Desportes' studio was purchased by the French king in 1784. In it one sees a silver soup tureen decorated with artichokes, the snouts of lions and a ducal crown. Around it are grouped a cruet, two silver sugar sifters and a basket of peaches. These objects are in the style of Thomas Germain, the famous silversmith, who was Desportes' neighbour at the Louvre, where both artists lodged, as did many other artists during the 18th century when the king was at Versailles. The aristocratic luxury of this still life forms a contrast with the bourgeois simplicity of Chardin's works.

SAMSON *(circa 1760)*: *Silver Ewer. Height: 26 cm. Museum of Decorative Arts.*

This piece, made in Toulouse, marks the end of the style known as rococo, with its curving lines and motifs derived from vegetation, which foreshadowed the *art nouveau* of 1900. At Paris there was a return to a more simple, classical style even before Louis XVI had ascended the throne.

Bodhisattva. Stone. China (End of 5th century A.D.). Height: 1.30 m. Cernuschi Museum.

This statue, coming from Yun-kang, in the province of Shansi, is a good example of the greatest epoch of Chinese sculpture, that of the Wei Dynasty. Its dominant virtues are the simple broad lines of the drapery, the calm nobility of the figure's attitude and the purity of its expression.

◄ *Persian Carpet (detail). Kashan or Kirman (16th century). Height: 3.75 m. Width: 2.70 m. Museum of Decorative Arts.*

The theme of the wild beast chase featured in this carpet is part of a well known tradition of Near Eastern art, appearing in Assyrian sculpture, Sassanid goldsmiths' work, and taken up again by the Mussulman art of Persia in its ceramic ware, miniatures and carpets, with great decorative elegance.

Dog. Terra cotta covered with a white glaze. China (Han Period, 3rd century B. C.). Height: 25 cm. Cernuschi Museum.

This example of the numerous funerary items in Han earthenware demonstrates the expressive power of Chinese animal art—in which Chinese artists of all periods excelled.

The Colossus of Rhodes. French Tapestry (beginning of 17th century). Height: 4.76 m. Width: 6.46 m. Gobelins Museum. ▶

This high warp tapestry has been woven in wool and silk enhanced by gold. It is part of the *Story of Artemis* series and was made on the basis of a cartoon by Lerambert to designs by Antoine Caron. This painter's subtle and elegant style is evident in the elongated figures and refined ornamentation.

Yeou. Food container. Bronze. Yin-Cheu style (11th-9th century B. C). Height: 17 cm. Width: 24 cm. Cernuschi Museum.

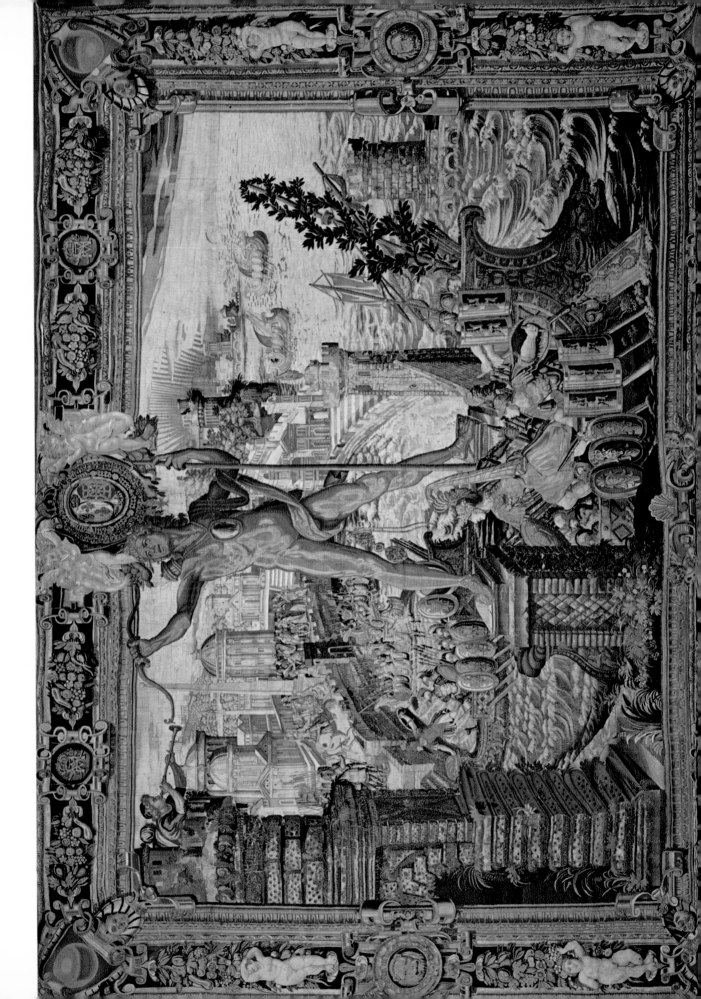

JEAN-BAPTISTE LEMOYNE *(Paris, 1704-1778): Bust of Young Woman. Terra cotta. Height: 41 cm. Cognacq-Jay Museum.*

This bust is thought to be of Mlle. de Vandeul, the sister of Diderot's son-in-law. Although he did not have the genius of his contemporary, Houdon, who became the greatest sculptor of busts in all France, Lemoyne lacked neither verve nor wit, as this delicate piece of work clearly shows.

MAURICE-QUENTIN DE LA TOUR *(Saint-Quentin, 1704-1788): La Présidente des Rieux. Pastel. Height: 1.16 m. Width: 95 cm. Cognacq-Jay Museum.*

A brilliant talker, frequently insolent to his sitters, even if the sitter happened to be the king himself, La Tour knew how to take the boredom out of sitting for him, so that his sitters maintained the natural expression for which his pastels are famous.

CLAUDE MONET *(Paris, 1840-Giverny, 1926)*: *Impression: Rising Sun. Canvas, 1874. Height: 45 cm. Width: 55 cm. Marmottan Museum.*

This painting is of historical significance, since it is the work which by chance gave birth to the term 'impressionism.' It was one of the works hung at the first exhibition of the young independent painters who had formed a 'limited company', an exhibition held in 1874 in the studios of Nadar, the photographer, in the Boulevard des Capucines. The public reacted violently to these canvases and in *Charivari* the journalist Leroy derisively referred to their painters as '*impressionnistes,*' taking the word from the title of Monet's painting. The victims of his criticism took up the gauntlet and accepted the name which was later to acquire honour and glory.

FRANÇOIS GÉRARD *(Rome, 1770-Paris, 1837). Portrait of Désirée Clary. Canvas. Height: 63 cm. Width: 52 cm. Marmottan Museum.*

A distinguished and exact portraitist of the notabilities of the First Empire, Gérard has painted here one of its most celebrated women. Désirée Clary married Marshall Bernadotte in 1798, after having been paid court to by Napoleon. She was destined to become Queen of Sweden.

VICTOR HUGO *(Besançon, 1802-Paris, 1885): My Destiny. Drawing, 1857. Height: 17 cm. Width: 36 cm. Victor Hugo Museum.*

Little known during the poet's lifetime, Victor Hugo's drawings are today regarded as works of art of the first rank. In no way the work of an amateur, they are the result of the assiduous study which Hugo carried on at various periods in his life, notably during his trips through Germany and while in exile. In this drawing his highly complex technique makes use of the pen, the ink wash and gouache. Yet the work owes its originality first and foremost to its grandiose inspiration. It shows us a boat caught in the spume of a gigantic wave, breaking beneath it. The audacity of the composition equals that of Hokusai's finest creations. Yet the work's significance lies in its symbolism, to which the title the poet gave it draws attention. It is this symbolism which raises this romantic work to the level of a universal classicism.

VICTOR HUGO: *The Eddystone Lighthouse. Pen, wash and aquarelle. Height: 89 cm. Width: 47 cm. Victor Hugo Museum* ▶

One of the most important of Victor Hugo's drawings, in which his imagination transforms a dilapidated ruin into a fantastic monument.

138

Victor Hugo 1866

JEAN-JACQUES HENNER *(Bernwiller, Upper Rhine, 1829 - Paris, 1905): Nymph beside a Spring. Canvas. Height: 40 cm. Width: 36 cm. Henner Museum.*

Henner's nudes, with their flowing red locks and their bodies bathed in a golden light against a dark background, enjoyed enormous popularity towards the end of the 19th century. But their glory has since faded.

GUSTAVE MOREAU *(Paris, 1826-1898): The Unicorns. Canvas. Height: 1.16 m. Width: 90 cm. Gustave Moreau Museum.*

This work, complex in its technique, which blends oil with distemper and water-colours, is every bit as complex in its subject matter, which unites traces of the *Dame à la Licorne* tapestry with the imitation of the Italian primitives and the literary symbolism in vogue in the *fin de siècle* years. The rich ornamentation in the form of materials and jewels does not obscure the purity and elegance of line. For some years now the Surrealists have re-established Moreau's importance after a period during which he was looked upon as decadent.

ANTOINE BOURDELLE *(Montauban, 1861-Le Vésinet, 1929)*: *Hercules as an Archer. Bronze. Height: 2.28 m. Antoine Bourdelle Museum.*

For this piece of statuary Bourdelle took Doyen-Parigaud, a captain of the cuirassiers, as his model. The captain was not able, however, to hold the pose for more than a few minutes at a time.

The " Soleil-Royal."   Ship's model.   Scale, 1 : 40.   Maritime Museum.

This splendid model of a ship belonging to the French Navy was constructed by the sculptor Tanneron, in 1839.   It gives an idea of the rich ornamentation of these men o' war in Louis XIV's day, covered with mythological figures, cornucopias, suns, and garlands.   The sculpture on this vessel is attributed to Coysevox.

JEAN-BAPTISTE OUDRY *(Paris, 1686-Beauvais, 1755): The King holding the Bloodhound at the Carrefour Puys Solitaire. Canvas, 1783. Height: 45 cm. Width: 35 cm. Nissim de Camondo Museum.*

This canvas is one of the eight sketches in this museum made for the tapestry of Louis XV's *Chasses royales*, commissioned in 1733 and woven at the Gobelins studio to designs which are now kept in the Châteaux of Fontainebleau and Compiègne. Here one sees a scene during the royal hunt, always one of the main pastimes of the French court and one which could sometimes have a diplomatic or sentimental significance. Was it not at one such hunt that Louis XV met Madame de Pompadour? This scene, in which the courtiers can be seen following the monarch at a respectful distance, is both lifelike and lively.

The Large Study on the First Floor. Nissim de Camondo Museum.

This reconstruction of a Louis XVI interior is composed of exceptionally fine pieces. Among them one distinguised a roll-top bureau in speckled mahogany, signed by the master-joiner, Claude-Charles Saunier; on the wall an Aubusson tapestry representing the Fables of La Fontaine to designs by Oudry, a fifteen-branched chandelier in chiseled bronze and gilt, a Bacchante painted by Mme Vigée-Lebrun and an Aubusson carpet in the de la Savonnerie style.

CLAUDE MONET *(Paris, 1840-Giverny, 1926):   The Water Lilies.   Lined canvas.   Height: 1.97 m. Width: 4.25 m.   Orangery Museum.*

The nineteen large panels in the *Water Lilies* series constitute one of the most important and homogeneous ensembles ever made by a modern French painter.   Through the intermediary of his friend, Georges Clemenceau, Monet gave them to the State, which had two rooms specially constructed for them in the former Orangery at the Tuileries.   These paintings were made during the 1914-1918 war, in the Giverny garden, which Monet had purchased in 1891 and where he had built a pool with water lilies.   He did a first series of canvases on this theme between 1898 and 1908.

Having undergone an operation for cataract in the meantime, he undertook another series in 1915, those at the Orangery. His composition has become broader and freer to such an extent that, isolating fragments of the painting or considering certain studies, critics have come to praise it as foreshadowing informal art, after having judged it for years to be senile and decadent. In these works Monet has given expression to the lyricism of nature, simple and uncultivated, and to a passion for light and a pantheism in which we detect above all a final and touching incarnation of romanticism.

'*Lion' Armour.   Chased and gilded bronze.   The work of Italian artists at the École du Louvre, circa 1540.*
Man-size. War Museum.

Suit of Armour belonging to François I. Chased and gilded bronze. Man-size. War Museum.

This suit of armour is the work of Jean Seusenhoffer of Innsbruck (1531-1540). Commissioned by the Emperor Ferdinand I, it was presented by him to the King of France. The chased work is extremely rich, featuring fleur-de-lys, sirens and flower-patterns in the pure style of the Renaissance.

The Course of Human Life or the Various Ages of Man. Engraving, 1825-1828. Height: 27 cm. Width: 36 cm. Museum of Popular Arts and Traditions.

This popular engraving is signed 'Feldtrape Fils', and the place of publication, Beauvais, at Dupont-Diot's. Here the life of man has been interpreted in a highly original manner by a dozen couples, from birth to the age of 100, 'the age of imbecility,' their prime being reached at the age of 50. On their death, the angel and the devil fight for their souls according to the medieval tradition.

◀ DOMINIQUE INGRES *(Montauban, 1780-Paris, 1867): Napoleon I on his Throne. Canvas. Height: 2.60 m. Width: 1.63 m. War Museum.*

Commissioned by the Legislative Council and put on exhibition at the Salon of 1806, this canvas has been the subject of lively criticism. 'Seems to have been painted in the moonlight,' wrote the Amateur of the *Lettres Impartiales*. However, although the portrait was not done from life and is rather cold, one cannot but admire the stylization of the materials of which the coronation robes are made and their excellent painting; also the truly imperial nobility of attitude.

Bottle. Stone with a salt varnish. (End of 18th or beginning of 19th century). Height: 25 cm. Museum of Popular Arts and Traditions.

This curious item of ceramic ware comes from Noron-la-Poterie, in the Calvados region. The stopper, taking the form of a person in a tricorn hat, with a dog-collar and a breviary, may represent a priest. It has been stylized, having severely shortened arms folded in front, like those of the old gods of Gaul. This may be an unconscious survival as is often found in popular art. The cherubs' heads are in the baroque style. The simplified floral decoration bears witness to that good taste which gives most of these works of traditional peasant art their charm and quality.

INDEX

ACKNOWLEDGEMENTS

Photographs by:

ARCHIVES PHOTOGRAPHIQUES: 54, 89, 96, 113, 115, 148, 149.
BULLOZ, Paris: 38, 39, 42, 43, 55, 60, 69, 101, 103, 104, 117, 118, 120, 121, 123, 124, 137, 138, 139, 144.
ETABLISSEMENTS BRAUN: 146-147.
GIRAUDON, Paris: 23, 28, 29, 30, 31, 32, 33, 34, 35, 37, 40, 49, 52, 57, 59, 63, 70, 82, 84, 88, 94, 97, 105, 108, 116, 131, 141, 142, 146-147.
HEROEG, Paris: 21.
ISTITUTO GEOGRAFICO DE AGOSTINI, Novara: 25, 26, 27, 48, 50, 51, 58, 62, 65, 68, 72, 74, 75, 77, 78-79, 80, 81, 83, 85, 86, 87, 90, 91, 92, 93, 95, 100, 102, 106, 107, 109, 110, 111, 112, 114, 119, 122, 132a, 132b, 134, 135, 140, 150, 151, 152.
L. LANIEPCE, Paris: 17.
MUSÉE DE LA MARINE: 143.
MUSÉE DE L'HOMME: 24.
MUSÉE DES ARTS DÉCORATIFS: 125, 126, 127, 128, 129, 130, 145.
JOSÉ OSTER, Paris: 22.
R. PASQUINO, Paris: 18.
A. G. PHOTO: 36.
LA PHOTOGRAPHIE UNIVERSELLE, Paris: 20.
D. RISCHMANN, Paris: 19.
H. ROGER-VIOLLET, Paris: 5, 6, 9, 10, 12, 15.
SCALA, Milan: 41, 44, 45, 46-47, 53, 56, 61, 64, 66, 67, 71, 73, 76, 98-99, 133, 136.

Printed in Italy by Istituto Geografico De Agostini S.p.A. - Novara - 1968
Imprimé en Italie - Stampato in Italia